HARD LYING

Hard Lying

The Birth of the Destroyer
1893-1913

PETER SMITH

NAVAL INSTITUTE PRESS

Library of Congress Catalog Card No. 73–88031

ISBN 0–87021–828–X

Published and distributed in the
United States of America by the
Naval Institute Press

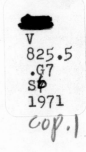
*Printed and bound in Great Britain by
W & J Mackay Ltd, Chatham, Kent*

Contents

Contents

7

List of Illustrations

Acknowledgements

This book, the first it is hoped of a series covering the whole history of the Destroyer in the Royal Navy, is the result of over ten years of research and accumulation of data and records. While it cannot compete with the more costly productions, this book does contain the details of the development of these splendid vessels, now alas almost all gone, in readable form.

Because the research behind this book has been spread over so long a period, it is impossible to give due recognition to every individual who gave me help, advice and assistance, so here I would like to thank all my friends, who share my love for destroyers, for their contributions, large or small.

Prominent among these over the years have been Jim David, Jim College, Edwin Walker and Walter Scrivener, all of the now defunct Warships' Records Club. The following firms have given me also every assistance: Messrs. John I. Thornycroft and Company, Vickers, Limited, and C. A. Parsons and Company.

Printed sources have naturally been drawn upon, especially for the earlier years, and I would like to express my indebtedness to the following: *A Sailor's Odyssey* by Viscount Cunningham of Hyndhope (Hutchinsons); *Endless Story* by 'Taffrail' (Hodder & Stoughton); *Flotillas* by Lionel Dawson (Neptune Press); *The British Destroyer* by Captain T. D. Manning (Putnams); *Alfred Yarrow* by Lady Yarrow (Arnold); *H.M. Destroyers* by Commander P. K. Kemp (Herbert Jenkins); and various articles, notes and reports from numerous publications including: *The Times*, *The Engineer*, *Marine News*, *Warship International*, *Brassey's Naval Annual*, and *Jane's Fighting Ships*, as well as letters and notes from many ex-destroyer men.

Finally thanks are also due to my publishers, Messrs William Kimber, for allowing me to indulge myself by writing a book for pure pleasure.

Rainham, Kent.
September 1971   *Peter C. Smith*

11

Chapter I

Cause and Effect

In the late 1860s the front-line strength of the Royal Navy—and indeed of every naval power of any importance—was to be measured in 'Ironclads', that is to say in the number of major warships, so called because in those days they had to be sheathed and encased in armour; they were the forerunners of the modern battleships. Judged by this yardstick of the number of 'battleships'—or their equivalent—British naval supremacy had not been challenged for over fifty years. But by 1870 the first of many startling changes had begun to affect the Royal Navy, changes which were, over the next fifty years, to rend the service with argument upon argument as the development of warships was subjected to alteration after alteration—after having been stabilised in its basic form for centuries. And far and away the biggest threat to the hitherto undisputed supremacy of the battleship was to be the torpedo.

The earliest form of weapon which might reasonably be classified as a torpedo was seen in 1585, when the Italian inventor Zambelli produced a flat boat, packed with explosives and a fuse. This device was actually used two years later when it was drifted down-river against a bridge over the River Scheldt at Antwerp. Fulton's experiments in the late eighteenth and early nineteenth century also deserve attention, although more closely related to mine warfare. The first torpedoes to carry the name were used in the American Civil War, when various primitive devices were mounted upon tiny craft and sent against opposing Ironclads with devastating results; a sobering shadow was suddenly cast over the big-gun ship. These devices known as 'Spar Torpedoes' simply consisted of an explosive charge affixed to the end of a long pole which was mounted in the bows of a small craft. The tiny vessel then manoeuvred, under cover of darkness, into a position where the charge could be detonated against the enemy vessel's water-line. A large hole here meant the loss of the ship, no matter what plate and protection she carried on her exposed upperworks.

A further improvement on this simple idea was developed by Commander Frederick Harvey, RN, and was named after him. His idea was for a steamboat to tow behind her a floating charge; she would then cross ahead of her intended victim at a higher speed, the towing line would be caught and the charge pulled into target's side by the victim herself, whereupon it would detonate with the same effect as the 'Spar'. Both these ideas, however, depended on a smaller, faster vessel being able to run within close range of a larger, more powerfully armed ship and, of course, the chances of this being achieved lessened as the development of gunnery, swivel mountings, turrets and so on advanced.

The advent of a real independently mobile underwater device came about with the experiments of a retired Austrian Navy captain named Luppis who put his ideas into practice at Cattaro in 1866. Luppis was certain that his device could revolutionise naval warfare but, being no engineer, he sought the advice of one Robert Whitehead, the English manager of an engineering works in Fiume. Despite the primitiveness of Luppis's invention, Whitehead was at once struck with its potential.

Luppis's original torpedo, however, although it moved under its own motive power, travelled on the surface of the water and was therefore easily visible. Its speed was very slow, so it could be avoided. Whitehead began experiments to perfect a self-propelled projectile with a heavy explosive charge in its head which would travel to its target *beneath* the surface, undetected.

The Austrian Government was very impressed and with its financial backing the Luppis-Whitehead torpedo was produced as a prototype in 1866; it travelled under water at 6 knots, carrying an explosive charge of 18 pounds in its head. It was driven by compressed air contained in a storage chamber and had a range of some 400 yards. The behaviour of this weapon was very erratic, and its depth-keeping varied from 5 to 15 feet. It was, however, a worthwhile beginning and Whitehead thus began to search for a solution to its erratic course-keeping.

By 1868 he had come up with a device to control the weapon's depth using a pendulum working in conjunction with a hydrostatic valve, actuated by the depth of water. He also increased the torpedo's capabilities by inserting a stronger airchamber with a pressure of 1,200 pounds per square inch, which gave his weapon a speed of 8 knots and an extra 300 yards range. It still remained unpredictable in its course-keeping, a fault which was to persist throughout the life of the weapon itself.

The propulsion unit of the Whitehead torpedo was carried abaft the warhead. The central section of the torpedo case contained a compressed-air cylinder which was the means of producing the necessary power for propulsion; behind this was a small engine compartment driving the screws. Early examples weighed around 35 pounds and were driven by the compressed-air jet.

The Austrian Government had by this time exhausted their supply of money in support of his programme and so Whitehead took his torpedo to the world's premier naval power for trial and evaluation. Although many have accused the Admiralty of backwardness in adopting new inventions, the charge cannot be levelled in this case, for a committee of officers from the Mediterranean Fleet under Vice-Admiral Paget was appointed and resulted in a hasty invitation for Whitehead to demonstrate his device in England.

At Sheerness a torpedo-tube was fitted in the bows of HMS *Oberon* and torpedoes were fired from it at a hulk moored in the Medway. The complete and swift success of these trials led to the British Government's purchasing the manufacturing rights of Mr Whitehead's invention for £17,000. More, they stipulated that the torpedoes were to be manufactured solely in England and they financed a workshop at Woolwich Arsenal to enable the weapon to be further developed and perfected.

A select number of officers were assigned to be trained in torpedo-construction and the Admiralty were, further, 'to be fully advised of all improvements and have the rights of using all such improvements', which meant complete control of Whitehead's torpedo.

Further developments took place at Woolwich and the adoption of oppositely rotating screws on the same shaft was a big step forward in stabilising its forward movement. The standard 14-inch diameter torpedo emerged, a weapon with 1,000 yards range, a speed of 25 knots and a warhead of 33 pounds.

Once the weapon itself was developed sufficiently to consider its general application, the problem arose of finding a suitable craft from which to launch it. Two fearsome vessels took the water in the following period as the Navy cast about for a solution to this problem. The first, HMS *Vesuvius*, was fitted to carry an outfit of ten Whitehead torpedoes on a displacement of 260 tons. She was an iron ship but her speed was a mere 9 knots and experiments to make her engines noiseless were not entirely successful. She was obsolete even on the day of her completion, in 1874.

Similarly her successor, HMS *Polyphemus*, described as a Torpedo-Ram, was singularly ill conceived. Ten times the size of *Vesuvius*, she combined a low freeboard, an enormous steel ram 12 feet long and a speed of 17 knots with an interesting combination of torpedo-tubes. She was fitted with a submerged bow-tube fitted underneath the ram itself. (Had the latter been used in combat the effects on the tube mounting can only be left to the imagination!) She had two tubes amidships; and two more mounted above the water in the hurricane deck completed the picture. She was immortalised by H. G. Wells as 'Thunder Child' in the *War of the Worlds*, but never saw action in her natural element. The key to the successful use of the torpedo lay in speed of approach, both by the weapon itself and, more necessarily, by the delivery craft. Alfred Yarrow, a young builder who specialised in fast steam launches, had, as early as 1873, mounted a spar torpedo on one of them.

With the arrival of the 'Whitehead' the governments of the world took notice of this new and cheap method of attaining equality with the larger and longer-established maritime powers.

A naturally alarmed Admiralty held firm to the view that the torpedo-boat was the 'weapon of the weaker power', a view they put forward with equal tenacity many years later with regard to the submarine. None the less, by 1877 with the British shipbuilders constructing fast torpedo-armed craft for a score of foreign navies they consented to purchase for evaluation one of Thornycroft's remarkable vessels which they named the *Lightning*. She was a steam launch of a mere 84 feet length and could achieve a speed of 19·5 knots; she originally mounted a spar torpedo but was soon modified to carry two Whitehead torpedoes in upper deck mountings. They also purchased two torpedo-boats from Yarrow's which were under construction for Russia; the Russo-Turkish conflict of 1877 had been greeted with a minor alarm in Britain and Yarrow was refused permission to allow his boats to sail. Instead the Admiralty agreed to purchase them. No one believed that speeds in excess of 18 knots were possible and the Admiralty stipulated heavy penalties in the purchase price should the Yarrow boats fail to meet the 18-knot standard set by his rival Thorny-croft.

Yarrow agreed to these conditions subject to an equally heavy premium being guaranteed for speeds *over* this figure. On trials being run the two boats turned in speeds of 20·8 and 20·6 knots respectively and the Admiralty was forced to part with an extra £1,900! Reporting on the Naval Review held in 1878 *The Times* of 14th August stated:

> One of the features of the Review was the performance of two long double-funnel torpedo-boats, built by Yarrow, which have realized the extraordinary speed of 21 knots. The manner in which these malevolent-looking craft rushed up and down the lines and round the ships was the astonishment of all beholders.

About a dozen of these so-called 'First-Class' Torpedo-Boats were constructed for the Admiralty by the leading builders of the day, but this initial impetus was soon lost. Parallel development over the next few years was the construction of large numbers of the smaller—and cheaper—'Second-Class' boats. Their function was to serve as tenders to larger ships and they were hoisted in and out of action by davits. To ensure light, easy handling qualities, they were constructed to dimensions of 60 feet length by 9 feet beam; lifting weight was 12 tons and their speed was 17 to 18 knots.

Meanwhile the development of the torpedo itself had con-tinued unabated all over the world, but the dangerous state of the British Navy's potential, a condition which applied as much to her battleship fleets as to her lack of torpedo-craft, was not brought home to the country until 1885. For five years warship construction had lapsed to an alarming degree.

It was a lecture given to the Royal United Service Institution in that year by Alfred Yarrow which first stirred the Government's conscience with regard to the lack of torpedo-craft in the Royal Navy, for it was revealed that, whereas Russia possessed no less than 115 of these craft and France fifty, Great Britain could muster no more than nineteen! A crash programme of fifty-four torpedo-boats was the result, but although this cured one problem, the other—the protection of the battleship—remained.

The awe in which the torpedo of that period was held is obvious in a remark of one First Sea Lord, Lord Northbrook:

The torpedo would be the most powerful weapon of offence, and would be able to dispose of the most formidable ships in the service of this or any other country.

Some felt, however, that this was merely an excuse for the Government to avoid a major battleship replacement programme— a ruse often repeated in this century, employing one pretext or another!

It must be remembered that the development of the quick-firing gun had not yet taken place. The cumbersome guns of the contemporary men-of-war were soon found to be totally inadequate to cope with the expected swarms of fast-moving torpedo-craft and much energy was devoted to the production of a rapid-firing gun.

Once various calibres had been tried it became the practice for all battleships to carry dual armaments. The big guns, the monsters of up to 18-inch calibre which fired one-ton projectiles for twenty miles, were known as the Main Armament. The smaller guns, capable of stopping the little torpedo-carrying craft, were carried around the superstructure above the decks, and later in casemates behind armour. As torpedo boats, and later destroyers, grew in size, so the calibre of this secondary gunnery was forced up to deal with them. By 1914 the battleships were carrying 6-inch guns for this purpose as opposed to 3-pounders in the 1880s and '90s. The much later arrival of the aircraft further complicated this process and for a time battleships were forced to carry both heavy and light subsidiary guns to deal with destroyers on the surface and bombers in the air. Not until the late 1930s was this dilemma partially eased by the development of a 'Dual Purpose' gun system which could be used against both forms of attack.

One anti-torpedo measure adopted straightaway was the use of heavy metal nets designed to either halt or prematurely explode the warhead; these nets were rigged on all battleships at much expense and labour, but the drag effect of these when steaming was enormous. Nevertheless the order 'Out Nets' passed into service and the great booms carrying these screens were a further encumberance on all heavy ships of the period.

The only light automatic weapons available, the machine-gun and the like, were just not powerful enough to provide a certain defence against the torpedo-boat of 1885. The only solution was the construction of a vessel fast enough to overhaul the torpedo-boat, and armed with weapons heavy enough for them to sink such craft. They must obviously be large enough to accompany the main fleet and must provide a stable gunnery platform. Although the imposing speeds of torpedo-boats fell off quickly in any sort of a seaway, they were improving in both size and performance; the Admiralty specification for their opponents called for at least 21 knots.

Already the way had been shown by White's *Swift*, a 125-ton boat with a speed of almost 21 knots armed with six 3-pounder guns. She was known in fact as our first 'Torpedo-Catcher'. The Director of Naval Construction at the time, Sir Nathaniel Barnaby, came up with a design which it was hoped would fill the bill for the Admiralty's request for a vessel to be 'as small as possible to be self-supporting'. This vessel was the *Rattlesnake*.

Launched by Laird in 1886, the first of a class of four, she displaced 525 tons and was armed with one 4-inch gun, six 3-pounder quick-firing guns and four torpedo-tubes—mounted one in the bow, one in the stern and two abreast the funnel. With a 2,700 shaft horsepower she was designed for 18·5 knots, a speed she slightly exceeded in trials and which, it was felt, would be sufficient to overhaul any torpedo-boat in weather. But in fact both she and her sisters were bedevilled by unreliable locomotive boilers and were constantly breaking down.

In April 1887 the *Rattlesnake* was tested exhaustively against the newly completed torpedo-boats at Portland. The results were not auspicious: in a flat calm her margin of speed was only two knots and in any kind of seaway she failed to 'catch' a single torpedo-boat! An interesting side-light was the performance of the torpedo-boats themselves; of the eighteen boats employed, eight broke down in a full-power trial. Lack of ventilation made them almost uninhabitable below-decks after an hour's steaming, while a study of these manoeuvres showed that to attack the Fleet in daylight with a mere 4–5 knot speed margin was tantamount to suicide. This was the first of several such exercises, the results of which were uniform and did much to strengthen the Admiralty's resolve that the threat of the torpedo-boat—although the catchers couldn't catch them—was an overrated one at sea; in inshore waters, however, they were held to present a grave threat to a close-blockading squadron.

In an effort to produce a vessel of the Catcher type which would reach at least 21 knots under forced-draught*, Sir William White at the DNC came up with the 'Sharpshooter' Class which were built by the Royal Dockyards but engined by private companies. Larger in every respect than the ill-fated *Rattlesnake*, they displaced some 735 tons, were armed with a pair of 4·7-inch quick-firing guns and five torpedo-tubes and were designed to develop 2,500 hp with 4,500 at forced-draught.

Again they failed to meet the requirements of the Board; all experienced difficulties with machinery and hull weaknesses and their average speed was a poor 19·5 knots, when current French torpedo-boats were making 22 knots on trials. The Admiralty now turned to private constructors to effect the cure and the result was the so-called 'Improved Rattlesnakes' of the 'Alarm' Class. Of 810 tons and with the same armament, the eleven vessels of this type were ordered in 1890. All had locomotive boilers save one, and all again failed to exceed 19·5 knots.

The one exception was the *Speedy* which was built by Thornycroft and fitted with water-tube boilers. This not only made her the first warship in the Royal Navy with three funnels, but meant that she alone exceeded her 20 knots, maintained it in some kind of seaway and was reliable in service. Apart from this one ship the Navy had spent six years and had constructed almost thirty vessels, none of which could do the task for which they were designed. The fault lay with the locomotive boilers, but before admitting defeat the Admiralty laid down a further class of five catchers, *Dryad*, *Halcyon*, *Harrier*, *Hazard* and *Hussar*. Again the displacement went up, to 1,070 tons, and they were longer and broader in the beam, but despite a potential horsepower of 3,500 none of them was good for more than 19·7 at forced-draught. Obviously failures, as were all their predecessors, this unhappy clutch of catchers was subsequently re-boilered with water-tube types and re-classified as 'Torpedo-Gunboats'; in this Naval limbo they survived through to the First World War when finally some suitable employment was found for them as fast minesweepers and depot ships. Admiral Fitzgerald summed up this unfortunate experiment:

They had been called torpedo boat destroyers or catchers, which

---

* Forced-draught is the system of utilising fans to increase the fires in the furnaces of the boilers, thus increasing fuel consumption and also increasing steam-power.

was a misnomer, as they certainly never could have caught a torpedo-boat and consequently could not have destroyed it.

Rear-Admiral 'Jackie' Fisher was at this time Third Sea Lord and Controller and it was to this forceful personality that Alfred Yarrow went in the spring of 1892 to tell him of what he had seen during a visit to French shipyards. He told Fisher that boats under construction there would exceed anything building on this side of the Channel. Speeds of 24, 25 and 26 knots were being achieved, while in Germany Schichau of Elbing had constructed a torpedo-boat which attained 27½ knots on trial. But France was our main concern: she had 220 torpedo-boats; Russia had 152 and Germany 143. The catchers had failed, but some solution was needed—and needed quickly.

When this news reached the Press there was a great outcry, especially when the French constructor Normand announced his intentions of constructing a 30-knot boat in the near future. Fisher was a man of action as was Yarrow. Would the Admiralty like something better? Yarrow asked, and he suggested that he be allowed to construct vessels which would surpass the French boats then building.

Yarrow suggested dimensions of 180 feet by 18 feet beam with 4,000 horsepower and Fisher set up a Committee to study these recommendations, at once directing the DNC* that the armament should be 'powerful' and the speed 27 knots. They were to be of much smaller displacement than the catchers, but armed sufficiently to blow the French boats asunder once overhauled.

The Committee was appointed in March and soon recommended a new type on the lines indicated by Yarrow, 'in essence a super torpedo-boat'. In June 1892 orders were placed with Yarrow for the first two. Oscar Parkes relates the story of how they came to be so named:

Fisher asked Yarrow what they should be called. 'That's your job,' replied Yarrow. 'Well,' said Fisher, 'we'll call them *Destroyers* as they're meant to destroy the French boats', and their original name of 'Torpedo-Boat Destroyer'—TBD—was in due course abbreviated to 'Destroyer' and has so remained.

And so began the Destroyer story.

* Director of Naval Construction.

Chapter II

The First Steps

The DNC's office laid down a tough list of conditions and penalties for the new craft and at first mooted the idea that the boats should be constructed in the Royal Dockyards—this despite Yarrow's information and assistance. Following their failure with the catcher design there was considerable opposition to this idea and one builder after another expressed dissatisfaction. Sir William White, however, took an opposing view to this idea and pointed out that only firms of specialist builders could give the hull and machinery that extra precision and attention which would be necessary to ensure that the hitherto unattained standard speed of 27 knots be reached.

Three firms stood out as meeting the stringent requirements for builders of such prototypes—Yarrow and Co of Poplar, London, John I. Thornycroft whose yards were also Thames-based at Chiswick, and the Birkenhead company of Laird Brothers. All submitted designs for consideration and the first contracts were awarded to these three firms, Yarrows being the quickest off the mark. As was the policy at the time, each builder was allowed considerable latitude in which to work within the general specification laid down, and the resulting boats differed widely in performance, appearance, design and expertise.

Yarrow's brace, the *Havock* and the *Hornet*, were historically important as the world's first destroyers. *Havock* was launched in October 1893 and her official trials took place on the 28th of that month. With dimensions of 180 feet × 18½ feet × 11 feet, she displaced a mere 240 tons, one-quarter the size of a catcher. Her armament consisted of a single 12-pounder gun mounted atop the typical turtle-back which was the distinguishing feature of all the torpedo-boats of the time. A 'turtle-back' forecastle, as the name implies was one with a raised, rounded shape convexly sloping to the upper deck level. This allowed the seas to fall away unhindered and facilitated the ship's passage—in fact, it was an early form of

streamlining—and was introduced with the earliest torpedo-craft.
It proved successful in smooth water, but was less satisfactory in
a heavy sea and could at times be dangerous.

Two 6-pounders were mounted abreast the 12-pounder platform
firing over a berthing rail, with another aft. Three torpedo-tubes
were mounted, two single 18-inch tubes aft with another in the
bow. The retention of the bow tube is interesting. This position
for a torpedo-tube had already been tried out in the torpedo-boats,
where it had been pronounced unsatisfactory. True it allowed for
an accurate sighting, but it caused navigational difficulties in a seaway casting up a permanent blanket of spray over the bridge. Such
an exposed position was also considered exceedingly vulnerable to
fire from light weapons and it was also found in the destroyers that
the boat tended to overrun the torpedo! It was therefore dropped
from all subsequent classes—only the first six prototypes carrying
them.

The bridge structure was merely a canvas screen erected around
the 12-pounder gun platform to the edge of the fo'c'sle stretched
on steel rods. The conning tower itself was protected by half-inch
plate, but the hull was less well served, being extremely fragile.
Three boats were carried, a dinghy on davits and two collapsible
'Berthon' boats. *Havock*'s two boilers weighed 54 tons altogether—
she was fitted with two of the locomotive type. Her near sister
Hornet shipped eight water-tube boilers, however—a great improvement which reduced weight to 43 tons and gave her four funnels
to cope with the additional boilers.

Cramming such enormous power into so frail a hull may have
gained the speed required, but life aboard was no sinecure; the
vibration at speed with unsynchronised engines was enormous,
while in the stokeholds it required non-stop stoking to hurl the
little boats through the water at 27 knots under forced-draught.
'The furnaces were of such dazzling whiteness that coloured glasses
were necessary when trimming.'

Hornet with her Yarrow water-tube boilers was certainly a great
step forward in small ship design and on 19th March 1894 she
attained a mean speed of 27·6 knots on a three-hour test. Yarrow's
boilers came through with flying colours, steam being raised from
cold to 180 pounds in twenty-two minutes. *Havock* ran her trials at
Maplin in a fresh breeze with the required 35 tons deadweight
insisted upon by DNC and reached 26·7 knots, the guaranteed

speed being 26. Her builders did not wish to push her too hard and only 3 inches of pressure was used in the stokeholds instead of the maximum 5. Nor was her bottom polished up with black lead as was common practice at the time to give that slight extra performance.

The Admiralty seemed satisfied, but not all opinion was initially lyrical about the new destroyer. For example *The Engineer* wrote of the trials:

> The disadvantages of this class of vessel are common to all Torpedo-boats and Torpedo Catchers—the upper part of the inverted cylinders, three on each side, being nearly flush with the upper deck, are dreadfully exposed to projectile fire from quick-firing guns. The size of the circular hatches prevents more than one man passing through them at the same time, and they must be duplicated, or in case of a collision or sudden foundering, half the crew below water will not be able to reach the deck. The conning tower is small, and the view therefrom is interrupted by the capstan on top of the turtle-back.

The trials of the first two boats attracted great interest and were widely discussed. *Hornet* especially triumphed during a tough course of trials on 23rd February when she emerged as the fastest vessel afloat. Twenty minutes after lighting fires she had steam and by the time she reached the mile posts on the Maplin course her engines were worked up to the necessary power and trials commenced right away. The commentator stated that the fact that there was 'no lack of boiler power was demonstrated by the violence with which the safety-valves were blowing'.

Complement for these tiny vessels was forty-two, a lieutenant in command, a sub-lieutenant, chief gunner, three chief petty officers, seven seamen and a signalman, with a chief engineer, a chief ERA, three ERAs, and twenty-three stokers for the engine-room complement. Accommodation for these men was described in contemporary records as 'sufficient but not luxurious', which was something of an understatement. The Captain of the *Havock*, for example, had no cabin at all! Commander Percy Brown, who commanded her in her latter days, used every ounce of ingenuity to achieve some measure of privacy. He boarded in his bunk and the space surrounding it, but to avoid cramping his companions in the wardroom a gap of a foot or so was left which was utilised by a wooden box beyond this area for the Commanding Officer's feet 'when in residence'.

The mess decks were crowded but adequate. Sanitation consisted of an open earth-closet erected when possible. The vessels themselves were steered from the break in the fo'c'sle with the steersman's head jutting out above the deck itself, while the officer in charge stood just beyond him and behind the gun itself. Attempts to steer these vessels at high speeds from this position were far from easy and after they had gone into service most vessels adopted a connecting device to the tiny bridge for conning from there.

Havock's coal capacity was 94 tons, which was placed in bunkers along each side of the boiler compartments; at just over 10 knots she steamed 44½ nautical miles per ton on early trials. Both vessels, *Hornet* and *Havock*, were accepted into the Royal Navy in 1893 at a contract price of £34,254 per ship of which the machinery accounted for £18,674.

In order to impress members of both Houses of Parliament with a view to financing further ships of this type, the First Lord of the Admiralty invited several influential politicians to watch Yarrow's boats carry out manoeuvres on the Solent. In June the *Havock* successfully overhauled and destroyed two 'enemy' torpedo-boats in exercises and completely outpaced the catcher *Speedy* off Portland.

Havock had a metacentric height of 2·48 feet which meant that she was a quick roller, her maximum righting moment being recorded as '48 degrees vanishing at 95 degrees'. Metacentric height is determined by the distance between the metacentre—the stable centre of the hull form—and the centre of gravity—determined by the vertical positioning of the superstructure, armament and so on; the height of this point determines the 'roll' of a ship and its steadiness as a gun platform. The vibration at 25 knots was worse than at full speed, although the reports from the Captains of the *Excellent* and *Vernon* establishments stated:

> The vibration and rush of wind through the sighting port in the gun shield was very disturbing to the gunlayer of the 12-pounder.

Certainly accuracy of fire was not among their attributes, but they proved time and time again that they could overtake the torpedo-boats and, at close range, were sufficiently equipped to overwhelm them, for the torpedo-boats themselves would be suffering the effects to a similar extent if not more so. The danger lay in the pursuit of the destroyer herself by protecting cruisers.

It became increasingly clear that the torpedo-boat destroyer, being more seaworthy, faster in normal conditions and more powerfully armed, was vastly superior to the torpedo-boat it was intended to destroy. It was soon realised that such vessels must certainly come to replace them in their primary task of torpedo attack. And so it ultimately came to pass; as the destroyer grew larger and even more powerful, its duties soon encroached, and then finally completely encompassed, those of the torpedo-boat. Not only were they to be required to drive the torpedo-boat from the sea but were soon called upon to follow this up by carrying out the torpedo-boats' role of attacking the main enemy fleet. In searching for an antidote the Admiralty had ironically constructed an even more potent threat to the battle-line upon which Britain still relied.

If any further proof were needed of the great superiority of the new type over her predecessors, then the Naval Manoeuvres of 1894 supplied overwhelming ammunition for the supporter of the destroyer. 'The Catchers', it was reported in *Brassey's Naval Annual*, 'with very few exceptions, were found to be quite incapable of acting as efficient catchers of torpedo-boats.' This failure was considered a very serious matter. Nor was the performance of the attacking torpedo-boats on the big ships rated very highly either. With the development of quick-firing guns proceeding apace, it was judged during the same manoeuvres that the swarms of torpedo-boats 'committed suicide in large numbers'. *The Times* Correspondent recorded that the work of suppressing the Blue Fleet's torpedo-boats had been mainly accomplished by the Blue torpedo-boats themselves and not by the Admiral in charge of the Red Fleet. 'They have suppressed themselves by their own temerity.'

Meanwhile at Chiswick Thornycroft's had put their first destroyer, the *Daring*, into the water. Fitted like *Hornet* with water-tube boilers of her builder's own design, she was of $185\frac{1}{2}$ feet in length with a breadth of 19 feet and 7 feet light draft. Displacement was 260 tons. Her three-stage compound engines were of novel design and Thornycroft introduced curved tubes in his boilers instead of straight; this was expected to prevent expansion strains, but in practice they proved to be difficult to remove for repair.

She ran her trials on the Maplin course and her engines performed satisfactorily enough, kept going by the boilers developing 4,800 horsepower, with steam at 250 pounds per square inch—'as far as can be judged from the needle of the guage, which is in a state of agitation with the varying velocity in the steam pipe'. Steam was raised from cold in fifteen minutes. An automatic system of feed was adopted, by means of a float in the upper drum regulating the opening of the feed pipe valve. This saved a great deal of anxiety among the stokers whose attention, it was recorded in *The Engineer*, 'are required elsewhere during the full speed trial'.

There proved very little vibration and the lack of any large bow wave or wake was considered remarkable, the wake being as flat and calm at full speed as at 15 knots. This smoothness was attributed to the Thornycroft form of stern. It was overhanging and flat underneath of full width which did not lend itself to the slamming effect at speed. The overhang space was utilised for the steam steering gear and the captain's cabin, while the propellers, being thus closed in, could be placed higher. With her draught aft thus reduced she would be able to pursue her torpedo-boat quarry into shallow coastal waters. *The Engineer* remarked further that:

> The larger size of the Torpedo Boat Destroyer as compared with the Torpedo-Boat enables them to maintain their speed much better in rough water, and to make it more difficult for a Torpedo-Boat to escape.

The *Daring*—and her sister, the *Decoy*—launched in August 1894, both utilised the special system of double rudders which gave them quite exceptional manoeuvring powers and enabled them to be steered astern as easily as ahead. But in official circles it was held that twin rudders gave no special advantages.

Trial figures for the *Daring* make interesting reading and show how the average speed was arrived at.

	Time	*Speed*	*Mean*
1. Against Tide	2 min 7·65 secs	28·214	
2. With Tide	2 min 6 secs	28·572	28·656 knots
3. Against Tide	2 min 3 secs	29·268	

Decoy with 4040 IHP reached 27·64 knots but was not pressed to her limit as her contract speed was only 27 knots. Both boats were tendered for £66,948 and this was accepted in June 1892 thus forcing both Yarrow and Laird to accept similar amounts for their respective braces of destroyers, although both had quoted higher figures.

The Laird boats, *Ferret* and *Lynx*, took to the water in December 1893 and January 1894 respectively. With dimensions of 195 feet by 19½ feet they were somewhat larger than their contemporaries, displacement being 280 tons. They had their engine rooms placed amidships between the double boiler rooms which was unique at this time. They were fitted with Normand boilers of the type in service in France which was acceptable to the Admiralty who wished to study this type in comparison with those of Yarrow and Thornycroft.

Trials were run in the Clyde, *Ferret* achieving 28¼ knots and *Lynx* 27 knots. With full bunkers of 80 tons of coal embarked their metacentric height was only one foot, or half what was considered desirable. Subsequent instructions that they were not to take on more than 60 tons of bunkerage resulted in a poor compromise, leaving them unstable and of short endurance.

Although all six reached their contract speeds and the 27-knot destroyer came into being, it must be noted that all these early boats ran their trials light, that is to say, with their torpedo-tubes landed, or reduced, to save top weight; specially hand-picked stokers trimmed the engines to coax an extra tenth of a knot from them. In fact the 27-knot figure was a purely artificial one and in service few of them ever attained it again.

In addition to running without armament on best Welsh coal, destroyers which took their trials over the Maplin course benefited by the fact that at speeds exceeding 25 knots the vessels mounted the accompanying wave of translation which could be worth an extra knot or even more on the registered figures.

The thin plating used to encase the bursting engines of the early destroyers was seldom more than an ⅛-inch thick and the ribbing of the frames and longitudinal struts could often be made out through it before successive layers of paint blotted them out. There was some doubt as to whether such fragile craft could survive the constant strains and pressures inflicted by their speed and the notable vibration of their engines. Alfred Yarrow, after much thought on the subject, eventually put his finger on the 'balancing' of the engines. In a paper to the Institute of Naval Architects in April 1892 he proved that it was in fact a lack of balance which caused the excessive vibration, rather than the effects of the propellers themselves. In conjunction with Dr Schlick of Hamburg, who was conducting similar experiments, Yarrow eventually produced balanced four-cylinder engines with their weights correctly disposed so as to eliminate vibration and these were universally adopted.

The superiority of the destroyer was so impressive that before they had completed their evaluation tests the Admiralty determined to place substantial orders for further vessels of this type. No less than fourteen firms were invited to tender over the next two years to construct a further forty-two 'Torpedo-Boat Destroyers'. In view of the rapid increase in the numbers of torpedo-boats joining the French squadrons on the Channel coasts this programme was passed, though not without some reservation, by the Board and Parliament, and even the two new super-cruisers, *Powerful* and *Terrible*, were delayed to permit their finance.

The decision to order from so many firms was astonishing, for only Yarrows, Thornycrofts and Lairds had any knowledge of the difficulties. But soon after their first destroyers had completed their trials Yarrows became aware that copies of the complete working drawings of their machinery were held by all the contracting shipbuilders. How this priceless information had been distributed to all their rivals was completely unknown to Yarrows, who saw only that all their research work had been passed on free of charge. In order to discover who had thus distributed their plans they placed an advertisement in the press as follows:

£200 REWARD

It having come to the knowledge or Messrs Yarrow & Co that COPIES of DETAIL DRAWINGS of the MACHINERY in H.M. Torpedo-Boat Destroyer *Havock* are being offered for sale, the above reward will be paid to anyone giving such INFORMATION as will lead to the discovery of the person so offering them for sale.

Poplar, London.

This quickly led to the Admiralty being revealed as the party responsible for placing the designs with the various firms, a practice which the shipbuilding profession held as 'incorrect'. Such high-handedness left Yarrow with absolutely no recognition for all the pioneer work they had undertaken in producing what was generally acknowledged as a first-class design for a new type. Nor did the Admiralty agree to acknowledge it until the matter was taken up in the House on behalf of Messrs Yarrow.

Finally on 15th August 1894, the Secretary of the Navy made an official statement to the House.

The Admiralty [he stated] are glad to recognize that Messrs Yarrow have been the contractors who had first constructed and completed with rapidity for the British Navy vessels of the high speed of the *Havock* and the *Hornet*. On behalf of the Admiralty, I am to express our satisfaction with the manner in which the contract has been carried out. We also acknowledge the value which we attach to the designs of Messrs Yarrow for the machinery of these vessels. Practical proof has been given of this favourable opinion by our use of certain parts of these designs as a guide to contractors for some of the other torpedo-boat destroyers since ordered.

Apart from this brief statement, Yarrows received nothing in the way of compensation. On the other hand the Admiralty ensured in future work that 'all drawings will be retained by the Admiralty', whether they were actually used or not for future designs.

So the way was clear for the rapid build-up of the destroyer force.

Chapter III

The 'Bloomin' Boats'

There were thirty-six destroyers in the first large batch ordered by the Admiralty in 1893. Time given to prepare designs was only six weeks, but all were launched in the period 1894–95 and the majority completed soon after. The displacements varied considerably as did the dimensions and the appearance of these vessels. The only thing common to all was the desired speed of 27 knots and an armament which for the most part comprised one 12-pounder and five 6-pounder guns, and two torpedo-tubes, the controversial bow tube being dropped in this and all subsequent classes.

Tonnages varied from 250 for the Yarrow boats, which were always designed to combine the greatest possible lightness consistent with strength—'cutting it fine' some people termed it—to the 320 tons of the J. S. White boats, *Conflict*, *Teazer* and *Wizard*. Their lengths varied between 190 to 208¼ feet, beam from 18½ to 20 feet and depth from 11½ to 13 feet. All save the Thornycroft boats, which had three-stage compound with twin screws, had triple-expansion engines and a single rudder. Coal bunkerage was between 60 to 75 tons giving them a radius of action of 850 to 1,350 nautical miles.

Boilerage was as diverse as the builders, with a resultant lack of similarity in speeds but they were all lumped together for classification as the '27-knotter' Class or, as it later became, the 'A' Class.

Yarrow water-tube boilers were fitted in the *Hardy*, *Haughty* (both Doxford), *Spitfire*, *Swordfish* (both Elswick), *Snapper*, *Salmon* (both Earle), *Opossum*, *Ranger* and *Sunfish* (all three Hawthorn) boats, while Yarrow's own three, *Charger*, *Dasher* and *Hasty*, were equipped with locomotive boilers—as were Hanna Donald's *Fervent* and *Zephyr* which were not successful. Both Laird and Thomson boats fitted Normand boilers, while Thornycroft and Fairfield had Thornycroft water-tubes. Barrow-built boats had Blychenden water-tubes, and the *Lightning*, *Porcupine* and *Janus* (all three Palmer) had Reed's. Whites fitted their boats with their own boilers.

Most of these boats managed their contract speeds, but some—as aforementioned—ran into difficulties. The problems attached to the construction of such specialised craft caused a few builders to burn their fingers. By far the most serious delays occurred with the *Fervent* and *Zephyr*. Single-funnelled, they were unique in profile, but try as they might Hanna Donald could not get them to the required speed. Trial followed trial and failure followed failure. Eventually they were both re-boilered with Reed water-tubes which gave them a four-funnelled layout, but which only just gave them the speed required to push them through their trials with figures of 27·1 (*Zephyr*) and 26·7 (*Fervent*) some five years late on delivery. As a result, the parent firm Hanna Donald never again tendered for destroyer work.

Whites also ran into difficulties with *Conflict* and *Wizard*, which were not delivered until July 1899. The *Wizard* was fitted with inturning screws, the only ship of her size to be so built. They caused her endless trouble in turning and at speed threw up an enormous wake. One of her later captains recorded:

The *Wizard* was a curiosity among destroyers. Built at about the same period as the *Salmon* and the *Bruiser*, she had been fitted with inturning screws, being the only torpedo craft thus afflicted. I say 'afflicted' because this feature made her extremely difficult to handle. For a technical reason the arrangement, which had been tried in various big ships, had been more or less of a success. But in the *Wizard* the propellers were so close together that they invariably worked in each other's disturbed water. This was all right as long as both were going ahead, but once either or both were reversed the fun began! To turn her by going ahead with one screw, and astern with the other required as much room as a battleship would take. To add to her drawbacks, she had a very small rudder.

Wizard was re-boilered in 1908 and reconstructed with two funnels, but even so the general opinion was that 'that infernal menace should never be allowed to move anywhere else than in the open sea, except in a flat calm, slack water, and with a tug in attendance'.

The Yarrow boats, together with their half-sister *Havock*, were

1. *Speedy*, the most successful of the Torpedo Boat Catchers, built by Thornycroft in 1893. The failure of the 'Catchers' led directly to the introduction of the 'Destroyer'

TABLE 1: The Prototypes

Six ships, completed in 1892–94 at an average cost of £33,474 per ship. Armament: one 12-pounder; three 6-pounders; and three 18-inch torpedo-tubes. Speed: best *Decoy* 27·7; worst *Havock* 26·1.

Name	Builder	Tonnage	Dimensions
Daring	Thornycroft	260	185½ × 19
Decoy	Thornycroft	260	185½ × 19
Ferret	Laird	280	195 × 19½
Havock	Yarrow	240	180 × 18½
Hornet	Yarrow	240	180 × 18½
Lynx	Laird	280	195 × 19½

Ultimate disposal: *Decoy* was sunk in a collision with *Arun* off the Scilly Isles in 1904; *Hornet* was sold in 1909; *Ferret* was scrapped in 1910; the remainder were sold in 1912.

2. *Havock*: built by Yarrow in 1893, she has been reboilered with three funnels. Note the bow torpedo tube and the turtle-back fo'c's'le

Ferret, built by Laird in 1893, passing battleships of the Channel Fleet. Compare her stern with that of *Daring,* Plate 5

4. *Hornet,* built by Yarrow in the same year with watertube boilers. The collapsible Berthon boat can be seen abreast of her funnels

6. *Sturgeon* after she had reached the fitting out dock of the Naval Construction Company in 1894

Thirty-six ships, completed in 1894–95 at an average cost of £35,780 per ship. Armament: one 12-pounder; five 6-pounder guns; two 18-inch torpedo-tubes. Speed: best *Boxer* 29·1; worst *Charger* 25·8.

Name	Builder	Tonnage	Dimensions
Ardent	Thornycroft	265	200×19
Banshee	Laird	290	$208\frac{1}{2} \times 19\frac{1}{4}$
Boxer	Thornycroft	265	200×19
Bruiser	Thornycroft	265	200×19
Charger	Yarrow	250	$190\frac{1}{2} \times 18\frac{1}{2}$
Conflict	White	320	200×20
Contest	Laird	290	$208\frac{1}{2} \times 19\frac{1}{4}$
Dasher	Yarrow	250	$190\frac{1}{2} \times 18\frac{1}{2}$
Dragon	Laird	290	$208\frac{1}{2} \times 19\frac{1}{4}$
Fervent	Hanna Donald	275	$200\frac{1}{2} \times 19$
Handy	Fairfield	260	$194 \times 19\frac{1}{2}$
Hardy	Doxford	260	196×19
Hart	Fairfield	260	$194 \times 19\frac{1}{2}$
Hasty	Yarrow	250	$190\frac{1}{2} \times 18\frac{1}{2}$
Haughty	Doxford	260	196×19
Hunter	Fairfield	260	$194 \times 19\frac{1}{2}$
Janus	Palmer	280	$200 \times 19\frac{1}{4}$
Lightning	Palmer	280	$200 \times 19\frac{1}{4}$
Opossum	Hawthorn Leslie	295	200×19
Porcupine	Palmer	280	$200 \times 19\frac{3}{4}$
Ranger	Hawthorn Leslie	295	200×19
Rocket	Thomson	280	$200 \times 19\frac{1}{2}$
Salmon	Earle	270	$200 \times 19\frac{3}{4}$
Shark	Thomson	280	$200 \times 19\frac{1}{2}$
Skate	Naval Construction Company	265	190×19
Snapper	Earle	270	$200 \times 19\frac{3}{4}$
Spitfire	Armstrong	280	200×19
Starfish	Naval Construction Company	265	190×19
Sturgeon	Naval Construction Company	265	190×19
Sunfish	Hawthorn Leslie	295	200×19
Surly	Thomson	280	$200 \times 19\frac{1}{2}$
Swordfish	Armstrong	280	200×19
Teazer	White	230	200×20
Wizard	White	320	200×20
Zebra	Thames Ironworks	310	$200\frac{1}{2} \times 20$
Zephyr	Hanna Donald	320	$200\frac{1}{2} \times 19$

Ultimate disposal: *Lightning* was mined in the North Sea in 1915; *Boxer* was sunk in collision in the Channel in 1918; *Ardent, Contest, Hardy* and *Shark* were sold in 1911; *Banshee, Charger, Dasher, Dragon, Hasty, Haughty, Hunter, Rocket, Salmon, Snapper, Spitfire, Starfish, Sturgeon* and *Teazer* were sold in 1912; *Hart, Janus* were scrapped in 1913; *Bruiser* and *Zebra* were sold in 1914; *Handy* was sold in 1918, and the remainder were sold and scrapped in 1919–20.

7. Hanna Donald's *Fervent* running trials in 1895—with her sister-ship *Zephyr* she was the only single-funnelled destroyer built for the Royal Navy until 1939

8. *Fervent* after she had been reboilered with four funnels—and had been finally accepted into the Navy

9. *Vixen*, built by Vickers, w

and huge ventilating cowls

TABLE 3: The '30 Knotters' or 'B' Class (Four Funnelled)

Nineteen ships, completed in 1896–1901 at an average cost of £60,000 per ship. Armament: one 12-pounder; five 6-pounders; two 18-inch torpedo-tubes. Speed: best *Wolf* 31·1; worst *Quail* 30.

Name	Builder	Tonnage	Dimensions
Earnest	Laird	355	213 × 22½
Griffon	Laird	355	213 × 22½
Kangaroo	Palmer	380	215 × 20¾
Lively	Laird	385	215 × 21¼
Locust	Laird	355	213 × 21½
Myrmidon	Palmer	370	215 × 20¾
Orwell	Laird	360	213 × 21½
Panther	Laird	355	213 × 21½
Peterel	Palmer	370	215 × 20¾
Quail	Laird	355	213 × 21½
Seal	Laird	355	213 × 21½
Sparrowhawk	Laird	355	213 × 21½
Spiteful	Palmer	365	215 × 20¾
Sprightly	Laird	385	215 × 21¼
Success	Doxford	380	210 × 21
Syren	Palmer	390	215 × 20¾
Thrasher	Laird	355	213 × 21½
Virago	Laird	395	213 × 21½
Wolf	Laird	355	213 × 21½

In the 1913 classifications all the 30-Knotters with four funnels were grouped as the B Class. Ultimate disposal: *Sparrowhawk* was wrecked off the mouth of the Yangtsze on an uncharted rock in 1904; *Success* was wrecked on Fifeness in 1914; *Myrmidon* was mined in the English Channel in 1917; all the others were sold and scrapped in 1919–21.

10. Cammell Laird's *Quail* of 1896 wearing her class letter

TABLE 4: The '30 Knotters' or 'C' Class (Three-Funnelled)

Thirty-eight ships, completed in 1896–1901 at an average cost of £60,000 per ship. Armament: one 12-pounder; five 6-pounders; and two 18-inch torpedo-tubes. Speed: best *Albatross* 31·5; worst *Dove* 29·3.

Name	Builder	Tonnage	Dimensions
Albatross	Thornycroft	430	$225\frac{1}{2}\times21\frac{1}{4}$
Avon	Vickers	355	$210\frac{1}{4}\times20\frac{1}{2}$
Bat	Palmer	360	$215\times20\frac{3}{4}$
Bittern	Vickers	355	$210\frac{1}{4}\times20$
Brazen	Thomson	345	210×20
Bullfinch	Earle	345	$210\times20\frac{1}{2}$
Chamois	Palmer	360	$215\times20\frac{3}{4}$
Cheerful	Hawthorn Leslie	355	$210\frac{1}{2}\times21$
Crane	Palmer	360	$215\times20\frac{3}{4}$
Dove	Earle	345	$210\times20\frac{1}{2}$
Electra	Thomson	350	210×20
Fairy	Fairfield	355	209×21
Falcon	Fairfield	355	209×21
Fawn	Palmer	360	$215\times20\frac{3}{4}$
Flirt	Palmer	360	$215\times20\frac{3}{4}$
Flying Fish	Palmer	360	$215\times20\frac{3}{4}$
Gipsy	Fairfield	355	209×21
Greyhound	Hawthorn Leslie	385	211×21
Kestrel	Thomson	350	218×20
Lee	Doxford	350	210×21
Leopard	Vickers	350	210×20
Leven	Fairfield	370	$209\frac{3}{4}\times21$
Mermaid	Hawthorn Leslie	355	$210\frac{1}{2}\times21$
Osprey	Fairfield	380	$209\frac{3}{4}\times21$
Ostrich	Fairfield	375	$209\frac{3}{4}\times21$
Otter	Vickers	350	210×20
Racehorse	Hawthorn Leslie	385	211×21
Recruit	Thomson	350	210×20
Roebuck	Hawthorn Leslie	385	211×21
Star	Palmer	360	$215\times20\frac{3}{4}$
Sylvia	Doxford	350	210×21
Thorn	John Brown	380	$218\times20\frac{3}{4}$
Tiger	John Brown	380	$218\times20\frac{3}{4}$
Vigilant	John Brown	380	$218\times20\frac{3}{4}$
Violet	Doxford	350	210×21
Vixen	Vickers	400	210×20
Vulture	Thomson	380	218×20
Whiting	Palmer	360	$215\times20\frac{3}{4}$

Ultimate disposal: *Chamois* sank in the Gulf of Patras, after her own broken propeller blade had pierced her hull, in 1904; *Tiger* was cut in half by *Berwick* in 1909; *Lee* sank in collision in Blacksod Bay in 1909; *Recruit* was sunk by *U.66* off Galloper Lightship in 1915; *Flirt* was sunk by German destroyers in the Channel in 1916; *Falcon* sank in collision in the North Sea, 1918; *Bittern* sank in collision with *Kenilworth* off Portland Bill in 1918; *Cheerful* was mined off the Shetlands, 1917; *Fairy* sank after ramming *UC.75*, which also sank, 1918; *Otter* was scrapped in 1917; all the others were sold and scrapped in 1919–21.

12. Thornycroft's *Albatross* at speed in the year 1908

13. Thornycroft's *Fame* of 1896 dressed overall at Hong Kong—in spite of her gleaming white paint she was a coal-burner!

14. *Otter*, built by Vickers in the same year, and also at Hong Kong. The handsome ship behind her is a French Cruiser!

TABLE 5: The '30 Knotters' or 'D' Class (Two-Funnelled)

Ten ships, completed in 1895–99 at an average cost of £60,000.
Armament: one 12-pounder; five 6-pounders; two 18-inch
torpedo-tubes. Speed: best *Ariel* 30·8; worst *Fame* 30.

Name	Builder	Tonnage	Dimensions
Angler	Thornycroft	335	210 × 19½
Ariel	Thornycroft	335	210 × 19½
Coquette	Thornycroft	355	210 × 19½
Cygnet	Thornycroft	335	210 × 19½
Cynthia	Thornycroft	355	210 × 19½
Desperate	Thornycroft	310	208 × 19½
Fame	Thornycroft	310	208 × 19½
Foam	Thornycroft	320(est)	210 × 19½
Mallard	Thornycroft	320(est)	210 × 19½
Stag	Thornycroft	320(est)	210 × 19½

Ultimate disposal: *Ariel* was wrecked on a Malta breakwater in
1907; *Coquette* was mined off the East Coast in 1916; *Foam* was
sold in 1914; all the others were sold and scrapped 1919–21.

. *Angler*, built by Thornycroft in 1897 and sister-ship to *Fame*—notice her funnel bands
d light-coloured upperworks

16. Destroyers moored at Dover at the beginning of the century—the picture brings out their high masts and frail construction

re-boilered in 1898 following the disappointing results of their locomotive boilers; the *Charger*, *Dasher* and *Hasty* received Thornycroft water-tube boilers and the *Havock* was fitted with Yarrow water-tubes. *Snapper* and *Swordfish* were both accepted at under contract speed, while the *Teazer* was seriously damaged on trials by the twisting of a shaft. Speeds continued to improve, however. The *Ardent* attained 29 knots, while *Boxer* logged 29¼ on a three-hour trial.

The *Handy*, *Hart* and *Janus* were sent out to the Far East but the majority of these boats served in Home Waters. As was traditional with all torpedo craft, they were painted black over all the hulls and turtle back, although a few had grey fo'c'sles. Boats in the East were painted white overall although exceptions were known. Their recognition pendants numbers were only painted up for manoeuvres.

Results of the 1894 Manoeuvres were still being analysed as these boats joined the Fleet. The *Havock* and *Hornet* had been assigned to Group 3 of 'A' Fleet for the Fleet Manoeuvres. Again the weaknesses of torpedo craft were stressed, and the two destroyers, regarded as Sea-going Torpedo-Boats, were said to be an overrated weapon and no ship was 'sunk' by them. One observer commented:

The Torpedo-Boats' strategic value is even lower than some of its most severe critics have placed it; and it is certainly not a little remarkable that they should be entertained at a time when some high authorities are beginning to doubt whether the position even of the battleship in the naval warfare of the future is not beginning to be imperilled by the development of vessels of the *Havock* and *Hornet* class, regarded as sea-keeping torpedo-boats, which might in favourable conditions attack even in daytime or, having found the enemy in the daytime, hover round out of range and attack in large numbers after dark.

The fact that they could remain at sea when normal torpedo craft had been forced to retire did make an impact in naval warfare, for up until then the torpedo had always been thought of primarily as a coast defence weapon; now it was rapidly becoming a dangerous offensive missile, the more so for the weapon itself was still undergoing improvement. The standard torpedo of the 1890s was an

18-inch diameter weapon, capable of 27 knots, with a rounded explosive charge.

Life aboard was a happy alternative to the stuffiness of the Victorian Navy and the appalling hardships were borne with cheerfulness by officers and men alike. To compensate the crews somewhat for the cramped conditions, lack of amenities and so on, 'Hard Lying' money was awarded, which for a lieutenant in command in 1908 amounted to two shillings a day. It cannot be held that they did not earn this money.

There was still considerable doubt as to how best to operate the destroyers once built and a special experimental squadron was formed with twelve destroyers, a like number of torpedo-boats and a pair of cruisers to try and reach some conclusions. It soon became apparent that controlling the concerted movements of so many high-speed craft was a task requiring great skill.

With hot coals falling about the decks, the wind and noise of the engines obscuring even shouted commands, it was bedlam aboard a destroyer. Their low freeboard and primitive equipment made station-keeping a thing of chance and maintaining contact with an 'enemy' fleet in heavy weather was found to be impossible.

In the Naval Manoeuvres of 1899, for example, the Admiralty expressly instructed the commander of the 'British' Fleet to use his destroyers—which he had based at Milford Haven, Holyhead and Lamlash—to obtain information relative to the workings of destroyers. They had instructed Admiral Dorville to employ his destroyers primarily for the attack and destruction of his adversary's torpedo-boats. The 'Enemy' torpedo-boats were stationed at Waterford, Kingstown and Belfast.

It is revealing to see how a destroyer rated in the rules laid down for the manoeuvres. A destroyer could put out of action a torpedo-boat at a range of a quarter of a mile, while *two* torpedo-boats could equally disable a destroyer at the same distance. Battleships, cruisers and torpedo-gunboats—as the catchers were by then called—could all disable a destroyer or torpedo-boat at 1,000 yards.

The 'Enemy' Admiral disposed his cruisers and torpedo-boats around his battleship force in such a manner that no destroyer could approach without theoretically being blown to bits, but his defence was never put to the test for the shadowing destroyers lost touch in heavy weather.

In view of the prevailing findings of such exercises the role of

torpedo craft was still very much in the air as the 27-knotters went
to sea. The only naval fighting which had taken place had been the
Sino-Japanese conflict of 1894, but even here no hard and fast
conclusion could be reached, the overwhelming Japanese naval
victory being due to the quick-firing gun.

> It is remarkable feature (wrote one contemporary observer) of
> the Battle of Yalu, and indeed of the whole war, that torpedoes
> have played so small a part in it.

It was left to the young men who manned these fragile, racing
craft to prove to their own satisfaction of what the destroyer was
capable. Although worked hard, these boats gave excellent service.
In October 1898 the *Surly* was selected for experiments with oil
fuel burning and was fitted with sprayers. The experiment was
more noteworthy for the clouds of evil-smelling smoke it produced than for any notable advancements, but in 1902 *Spiteful* was
similarly taken in hand. The *Havock*, minus most of her armament,
served for several years as Captain (D) in the Plymouth Port
Flotilla under the command of Commander Brown in company
with such senior citizens as *Daring* and *Lynx*.

By the early 1900s some of the old boats had deteriorated badly
and the *Skate* was the first of the destroyers to be taken out of
service in November 1905; she was used as a target at Shoebury-
ness until totally unfit and then sold out in April 1907 for £305!
Others followed as the cost of keeping them running outweighed
their usefulness,* but the *Ferret*, considered worn out in 1907, was
then re-employed as a 'Boom-jumper' for her engines were still
sound. She was driven hard at an experimental boom in Portsmouth harbour under command of Lieutenant Hodgson. Apparently she merely 'rode' the boom without a check in her speed,
although what conclusions were subsequently reached is not
known. Her fore-bridge, 12-pounder and bow-tube were removed
and the turtle-back strengthened for these trials, but she was sold
out in 1911.

The *Ardent*, *Bruiser*, *Banshee* and *Dragon* spent some time in the
Mediterranean. The *Salmon* was sunk at Harwich by the steamer
Cambridge on 2nd December 1901. She was subsequently salvaged
and served for a further ten years. On the outbreak of war most

* See Table 2, on page 38.

had gone to the breakers, although *Boxer, Conflict, Fervent, Lightning, Opossum, Porcupine, Ranger, Sunfish, Surly, Wizard* and *Zephyr* still survived as the 'A' Class veterans. They were used on coastal patrol work and apart from the two losses the others, completely worn out, went to the breakers in 1919–20.

Alfred Yarrow was convinced that the good results obtained with his first boats could be improved upon utilising the new 'Yolla' metal—high-tensile steel—which had a strength of 35 tons per square inch as opposed to 28 tons with mild steel. This stronger material permitted an appreciable reduction in the thickness of the hull, which helped towards the extra margin of speed necessary for a 30-knot design. He offered his ideas to the next Admiralty tender but met with indifference. However, the Russian Navy was more impressed and ordered a destroyer on the lines Yarrow indicated. This was the *Sokol* and she became the first vessel in the world to exceed 30 knots.

The increase of speed attained by successive torpedo craft in the last quarter of the nineteenth century was only made possible by the devotion of the specialist firms and the engineering advances which followed work by firms like Normand, Thornycroft and Yarrow.

To illustrate how resistance is augmented as speed is increased it is stated that to drive a vessel at twenty knots as compared with the same vessel driven at ten knots, *eight* times the power is required and this ratio increased proportionately for thirty and forty knots. Yarrow himself attributed the high speeds reached over such a short period to four main points:

(1) Increased revolutions of the machinery, and the higher pressure of steam.
(2) Introduction of forced-draught.
(3) The water-tube boiler.
(4) Adoption of steam turbines.

In other words the reduction of weight counted for much, all of which was in accordance with Froude's Law and meant that at a certain point there was no advantage from increased power if it meant increased dimensions.

The success of the *Sokol*, and the French *Forban*—which maintained over 31 knots over a one-hour trial in 1895—led to a reappraisal of their 27-knot limit by the Admiralty and on their next order they set their sights on 30 knots as the average figure and wrote confidential letters to Laird, Thornycroft and Yarrow for designs. These were the first beginnings of a further huge destroyer construction programme which was later to be classified into four groupings or 'classes', the '30-knotters'.

Chapter IV

Rapid Expansion

The vessels built under the Estimates of 1894, and for the following two or three years, were generally a repeat of the first boats of the 27-knotter variety, but in view of increasing dismay at the speeds achieved by foreign torpedo craft, a 30-knot top speed was aimed at. Increased dimensions allowed for a modest improvement in amenity and the bridges were extended aft to enclose the wheel and binnacle, although the conning tower below still served in action as before. Some service opinion was in favour of a stronger hull, for grave fears were being expressed about the frailty of the earlier destroyers. A more robust and seaworthy hull could only be achieved, however, at the expense of speed and upon this the Admiralty were adamant. Inch-thick plate had been given to the Japanese destroyer *Kotaka* built by Yarrow, but such protection meant the loss of $1\frac{1}{2}$–2 knots and so was ruled out.

Although some small increase in size was allowed for, and the boats steadily grew in size through the period 1895–7, all the '30-knotters' were still extremely wet, and downright uncomfortable in any sort of heavy weather. On top of this, their contract speeds were seldom, if ever, reached after their trials, it being estimated that the '30-knotters' were never good for much more than 23 or 24 knots in general service.

Another factor which arose at this time was that of endurance; with the destroyers being more and more thought of as sea-going torpedo-boats, their endurance was, increasingly, as important as speed if they were to accompany the fleets abroad.

> These vessels [it was reported] are required to make a three-hour trial at full power, for continuous speeds, as well as a corresponding trial to ensure that the coal consumption does not exceed the limit set of 2·5 pounds per unit of power.

The *Mallard*, with 2·08 pounds per IHP per hour, came out best of the 30-knotters. A brief comparison is of interest between the various boats:

Builder	Ship	hp	Speed	Lb/IHP/Hour
Palmer	*Leopard*	6,848	30·135	2·299
Palmer	*Spiteful*	6,596	29·901	2·32
Vickers	*Otter*	6,265	30·274	2·490
Thornycroft	*Cygnet*	6,077	30·375	2·229
Hawthorn	*Cheerful*	5,566	29·941	2·840
Laird	*Orwell*	6,445	30·282	2·670
Fairfield	*Leven*	6,201	30·201	2·095

On the speed trials the *Wolf* achieved 31·107 knots and came out the fastest while *Dove* was accepted at 29·398 knots, but most of the others only achieved their contract speed by the narrowest margin. Failures to achieve the minimum requirements were common and some of the smaller firms like Thomsons and Earles were finished because of the costs involved in improvement, although Admiralty policy was not to exact the stringent penalties for such short-comings laid down in the contracts due to the experimental nature of this type of work; their Lordships were anxious to encourage as many firms as possible to attempt the work in order that a large force of destroyers could be built up as quickly as possible.

Again every leeway was afforded to individual constructors within the broad specification; over a period distinctive 'trade-marks' came to be associated with the designs of different firms and made them far easier to distinguish than the subsequent adoption of funnel bands and pendant numbers soon after 1910.

Yarrow boats were always of minimum dimensions to achieve the maximum speed; Hawthorn Leslie boats were reputed to contain small extras for comfort. But the number, size and positioning of the funnels was, perhaps, the most distinctive feature in determining the identity of these early destroyers. Palmer's boats had four funnels, with a rim sported just below the funnel top, and their early boats were fitted with funnel caps which were designed to prevent the sea entering the space between the uptake and the outer casing of the funnel—although Captain T. D. Manning, in his excellent work *The British Destroyer* says that this might alternatively have been to prevent rain and sea-water washing the soot from the funnels down the casing.

Laird's also utilised four funnels, but whereas Palmer boats had the second and third close together, Laird's were more evenly spread. Clydebank-built destroyers of this era had tall funnels, while Fairfield and Barrow kept them short; these short funnels had later to be raised as the smoke interfered with navigation and made the bridge untenable. This was a point not apparently taken by Admiral Fisher, who, when he was later responsible for ship design, would not tolerate tall, or even medium-sized, funnels on any of his vessels.

The early torpedo-boats had been fitted with the standard loco-motive boiler and this practice had continued with the introduction of the destroyer. The simple reason for this is that, for the desired ratio of boiler-weight to steam generated for speed, the loco-motive boiler in combination with forced draught produced the best results, but because of the peculiar differences in the applica-tion of locomotive boilers at sea they were never, even at their best, a very reliable form of power. Fresh water being unavailable, the only water suitable—sea-water is useless because of its salt content—is that which has already passed through the engines and been condensed. In the process a certain amount of grease is picked up which settles on the inside of the boiler. Being non-conducting, it forms after a time a thick enough film to cause distortion and overheating, sometimes with fatal results.

Due to the employment of forced draught, another hazard of locomotive boilers was the continuous shower of hot coals which poured from the flaming funnels of the early torpedo-craft. This was because the coal was often blown straight from the fire into the tubes before being completely consumed. Small wonder, then, that in early torpedo-boats and destroyers the first question on return to harbour was: 'How's the boiler?'

Because of this constant threat of distorted and leaking tubes, much consideration was given by the various shipbuilders to the construction of a satisfactory water-tube boiler. As is usual in such conditions, several firms came up with similar solutions at the same time and it became Admiralty practice to fit various differing makes to destroyers of the same type in order to gain a sea-going com-parison. The advantage of the water-tube boiler was that it could stand the heavy firing so necessary as speeds were required to rise by leaps and bounds. They were lighter and more reliable, and steam could be raised more speedily; free circulation and ease of cleaning were additional benefits. Water-tube boilers are con-structed so that the tubes are, in effect, reversed. The water from which steam has to be generated is inside the tubes, which straddle the furnace, and the hot gases and flames are outside. This allows for a more regular and rapid circulation, avoiding thereby the risk of overheating, and is a generally more reliable mechanism.

The first water-tube to be adopted was the French du Temple which was fitted to French boats in 1879; other pioneers were Yarrow, Thornycroft and Normand.

Again there was a diversity in the boilers fitted to the various boats; the Palmer boats had Reed water-tubes; John Brown, Thomson and Laird brothers the French Normand; Doxford, Earle, Fairfield, Hawthorn Leslie, Thornycroft and Vickers had the Thornycroft water-tubes; Hawthorn Leslie fitted these to their *Cheerful* and *Mermaid*, but fitted the Yarrow design to *Greyhound*, *Racehorse* and *Roebuck*.

As was to be expected, their performances differed widely. The designs were to some extent revolutionary and rapid expansion of numbers was also a factor which led to extreme difficulties when flotilla organisation came in. With boats of differing endurance, turning circles, speeds and weather service it was a headache for Captains (D) to run their boats, or even to maintain them.

Fisher was Vice-Admiral in the Mediterranean in 1900 and was full of enthusiasm for the destroyers themselves. Commenting on the Manoeuvres of that year he wrote:

> The destroyers all dashing about like mad in the middle of it all and torpedoing everyone! It is the best thing I have ever seen and most realistic.

He was not enamoured, however, of the complex problems of organising these hotch-potch flotillas:

> . . . a multiplicity of designs by eleven different builders . . . so many types on this station that *Tyne* [the depot ship] has to carry fifty tons of spare gear more than she need have done owing to differences in boiler tubes, propellers and all spare parts of machinery. Only two of the boats that came out last May are similar.

The Thornycroft boats were built with high-tensile steel, as had been suggested earlier, to save weight by thinner plating of the same strength. The weights of machinery varied considerably. The masting was the same as in the 27-knotters but most of the later destroyers had their Berthon lifeboats replaced by Reindeer hair boats, which were not popular.

This was still the Victorian Navy and much of the pomp and ceremony which so prevailed in the main fleets managed to filter down even to the new breed of the destroyer men. Strict regulations were laid down for the correct colour schemes for destroyers and the then-Sub-Lieutenant Andrew Cunningham described what this meant in the Mediterranean:

> She [*Locust*] burnt coal, and two of the funnels were fairly well aft. We were painted white and, when steaming, cinders were vomited onto our spotless quarterdeck. Destroyers of those days were delicate craft, and it took a lot of work to keep them running and efficient. It was harder still to keep them clean, and Dutton [Lieutenant Dutton] always insisted upon the corticene decks being as white as a hound's tooth and all the brightwork being polished and shining. I remember that our funnels and upperworks were grey, ours being painted with a special grey wash made from a recipe the secret of which was known only by our Chief Stoker. He was like one of the witches in *Macbeth* over her cauldron when he boiled it up while murmuring incantations.

In an effort to alleviate the apalling effects of rolling in these small vessels experiments were conducted with the fitting of internal tanks along the ships bottom—or bilge-keels. The *Star* was so converted at a cost of £250 and this proved successful enough to bring about the eventual fitting of bilge keels in subsequent classes.

In order to ease the duties of the stokers who had to work under terrible conditions forced lubrication of the engines was introduced with the *Syren* in 1899 and this was a marked improvement. The previous common failing of bearings running hot and having to have sea hoses played on them was almost entirely eliminated. The life of the stoker was not one to envy in the early boats and it is a thousand wonders that men withstood so much, scalded by the steam, deafened by the roar, bucketed by the pitch and roll of the little ships with only a paper-thin sheet of steel between them and the racing sea. The complexity of the machinery and its unreliability ensured no lack of diversity in the engine rooms of the TBDs. As one observer was later to write:

The great trouble in the older destroyers was to keep up at high speeds the water supply for the numerous small boilers with which they were fitted. In the *Salmon* we had eight water tube boilers, which seemed an excessive number for a ship of 300 tons. The engineer always used to say that the last two or three of these only made the deck hot, since the engines could not take the steam from them, even had they been able to keep up the supply at anything approximating to high speed.

It was no wonder then that during exercises in 1904 no less than sixteen of the 30-knotter destroyers broke down or reported faults; one boat, the *Violet*, had to be towed 120 miles after her boilers burnt out. Nevertheless the 30-knotters were sufficiently successful for them to be taken as the prototype for destroyers all over the world and their like served in the navies of Japan, Russia, France and Germany for many years. Although frail in build the punishment they were subsequently able to take was enormous and many of them survived to serve right through the Great War. Used hard in manoeuvres by men like Lewis Bayly, who were determined to bring their boats up to fighting pitch no matter what the risks, the boats soon began to suffer casualties, which was not at all to the liking of the Admiralty. Bayly was right, of course, and the skill and self-reliance instilled by absolute realism was to produce in the young men of the destroyer breed an inbuilt aggressiveness and resourcefulness never equalled before, and which gained its end in the magnificent results achieved in both World Wars. The general view of the main fleets, however, was that destroyer men were little better than legalised pirates!

In service they were hard worked and some casualties resulted. The *Thrasher* was involved in a severe collision, soon after her completion, with the *Lynx*. She ran hard aground at Dodman Head at twelve knots and had to be re-boilered but she was never worth more than 25 knots after this although she remained in service. The *Syren* also ran aground during night exercises at Berehaven, 1st May 1909, and was rebuilt with a new bow section. The *Sparrowhawk* was sunk in June 1904 after striking an uncharted rock off the mouth of the Yangtse River while even more bizarre was the loss off Cape Papas in the Gulf of Patras of the *Chamois*; one of her propeller blades broke off while she was running a trial, flew up with the motion and ripped the destroyer's hull open.

In 1902 the cruiser *Pioneer* struck the *Orwell* and cut the destroyer in half. The bridge and fo'c'sle were lost and the repairs took eighteen months. This was followed by similar disasters when the *Attentive* crushed the *Quail*'s bows on 6th August 1907 and the *Tiger* went down with the loss of thirty-six officers and men after being rammed by the *Berwick* on 2nd April 1908.

Nor was this the end of the tribulations suffered by the 30-knotters. The *Crane* was in collision with the steamer *Princess Margaret* in March 1910; the *Lee* was written off after driving ashore in Blacksod Bay October 1909 and the *Bittern* and *Falcon* were both sunk in collisions during the war.

Apart from these heavy peacetime casualties only routine duties occupied the time of the new destroyers. A bright interlude occurred during the Boxer Rebellion of 1900. In this unusual setting one young destroyer commander at least had the satisfaction of taking his craft into action against an enemy destroyer, if only in an oblique fashion!

With the foreign diplomatic enclaves besieged in Peking it had been decided to mount an international expeditionary force to relieve them. As a prelude to this a fleet of warships from the various interested countries was assembled off the mouth of the Pei-ho River opposite Taku, which contained the only telegraphic link with Peking. Taku was strategically placed at the mouth of the river which was the easiest link with Tientsin and this in turn lay on the line of march of the relieving columns.

To seal off this line of communication and advance the Chinese had two powerful forts, one on each bank, in which were mounted sixty or seventy guns of heavy calibre, mainly Krupps' ordnance with German-trained gun's crews. There were also four modern destroyers built for the Chinese Navy by Schichau of Elbing in 1898; the Chinese had moored these ships close by the forts so that their 3-pounder guns and torpedo-tubes also commanded the river mouth; they were being used, in effect, as extra fortifications.

When word came that the Chinese were mining the river, the Commanders of the International Fleet issued an ultimatum to the forts, which was rejected, and the 8-inch guns of the forts started firing on any ships which ventured into range. With the International Fleet were two British destroyers, the *Fame*—commanded by Lieutenant Roger Keyes—and the *Whiting*.

Keyes was even then showing the qualities of dash and daring-do which were later to make his name a by-word and he put forward to Sir James Bruce a plan to seize the four Chinese destroyers in true 'cutting-out' style. After some discussion Keyes was given the go-ahead.

The Chinese ships lay moored in line-ahead and the *Fame* and the *Whiting* approached them under shell-fire, each towing a whaler full of armed seamen in the manner of Nelson's day. Keyes's command ran abreast of the first Chinese vessel, while the *Whiting* slipped alongside of the third, their armed parties taking the second and fourth. The Chinese seamen showed little inclination to fight and after a very brief skirmish all four boats were taken. The four captured destroyers were then taken up river out of range of the forts. It is of interest to note that one of these vessels, named the *Taku*, was taken over by the Royal Navy and served for many years, based at Hong Kong, until she was sold in 1916.

Keyes's thirst for action brough the *Fame* into the public eye shortly afterward for he deliberately disobeyed orders which forbade him to provoke action and, with a landing party of thirty men, he captured the Hsi-Cheng Fort further up river and blew it up! He was awarded fifteen pounds for the capture of the four destroyers but sent home for his exploit with the fort. En route for Hong Kong with the *Taku*, the *Fame*, running low on coal, was caught by a typhoon just outside. After some hair-raising hours on a lee shore with his command leaking after such a severe buffeting, Keyes managed to bring his command and his prize safely in.

Apart from the *Fame, Whiting* and *Sparrowhawk*, the *Virago* also went out to China but the majority of the other 30-knotters spent their time in home waters or in the Mediterranean.

*   *   *   *   *

The sixty-four surviving 30-knotters all served in the Great War although with extra equipment and crew. Feeling their age by then, they were hard pressed to keep running; that they did so, and with notable valour, says much for their designers, builders and crews, although it was only dire necessity and need that kept these tiny boats in action, their main theatre being the Dover Straits where at any time they could expect to come up against the most modern German ships.

Despite their age and size they are credited with the destruction of three U-boats.

The first success was achieved by the crippled *Thrasher* under the command of Lieutenant E. M. Hawkins, RNR. On 8th February 1917 she sighted a submarine—it turned out to be *UC.9* in the act of sinking a ship off Flamborough Head. Although *Thrasher*'s full speed was less than twenty-five knots and the submarine dived at once, Lieutenant Hawkins fired a single depth charge which was so accurate that it smashed open the German ship's conning-tower, flooding both it and the control room. The crew panicked and, due to the damage, the German captain had no choice but to come to the surface and surrender.

Thrasher opened a heavy and accurate fire when the submarine surfaced, killing the captain. A British prisoner aboard the submarine had the initiative to wave a white handkerchief, otherwise the submarine would have been blow to bits. The German U-boat was taken in tow by another destroyer, but subsequently sank.

The *Gipsy*, with the assistance of some drifters, sank the *U.48* by gunfire near the Goodwin Sands on November 24th that same year. The most gallant episode was the fight of the *Fairy* against the *UC.75* on 31st May 1918, again off Flamborough Head. She was under the command of Lieutenant G. H. Barnish and senior officer's ship of a convoy escort consisting of an armed whaler and six trawlers which were guarding a convoy of some thirty merchantmen. At 0200 the convoy had just rounded Flamborough Head and the *Fairy* was in position 'to seaward and a little abaft the beam of the rear ship of the convoy'. In such a position Lieutenant Barnish felt that whatever the emergency he would not have to waste time reversing course.

The night was overcast and dark, the sea was smooth and visibility was good. Due to the shoals in this area nobody expected an attack but at 0205 one of the convoy was apparently torpedoed. The alarm was sounded aboard the *Fairy* and full speed was ordered at once. Almost immediately a submarine was sighted on the port bow some 300 yards away. Despite the speed of the events Barnish was clearheaded enough to realise that in such a position it might very well be an English submarine and he flashed a challenge to her as the destroyer rapidly diminished the short distance which separated them. He aimed for the submarine's stern in order to minimise the damage in case the submarine was not hostile, but as the range came down to point-blank they could hear cries in German.

At full tilt the little 350-ton destroyer passed over the stern of the U-boat but without enough impact to damage it. Lieutenant Barnish determined to renew the attack and, opening fire with the after guns, the *Fairy* turned in a tight circle. The after 6-pounder exchanged fire with the submarine, scoring several hits.

It is now known that the first torpedo alarm had in fact been the submarine colliding with one of the ships of the convoy accidentally and after receiving the second blow from the destroyer with the prospect of a third in the offing, the German crew abandoned ship. Again at full speed the *Fairy* struck the *UC.75* firmly and with an appalling crash came to a standstill.

The submarine was in fact larger than the destroyer and the *Fairy*'s bows just could not stand the shock, crumpling like tinfoil as far back as the bridge. The submarine sank and the destroyer was left in a sinking condition with her head, or what remained of it, well down. The *UC.75*'s captain had managed to scramble aboard during the impact and surrendered himself.

Efforts were made to reach the shore to beach the little ship, but after her forward bulkheads gave way this could only be done by steaming stern first. Before long her propellers were airborne which brought the attempt to an abrupt conclusion; the engines were stopped and the crew took to the boats. At 0305, exactly one hour after the initial alarm, the little destroyer slid to the bottom in 16 fathoms. The crew and the submarine survivors were later picked up by the *Greyhound* and fittingly Barnish received the DSO for this action.

On the other side of the score sheet the *Recruit* was torpedoed and sunk with the loss of thirty-nine officers and men on the 1st May 1915 near the Galloper Lightship. Other destroyers fell victim to mines. The *Coquette* was sunk by mines off the East Coast on 7th March 1916; the *Myrmidon* in the Channel on 26th March 1917; and the *Cheerful* went down off the Shetlands on 30th June the same year. Yet others were lost through accidents. The *Bittern* was rammed by the steamer *Kenilworth* on 3rd April 1918. The accident occurred in dense fog and her crew never had a chance—the destroyer going straight to the bottom at 0315 with every man. Just two days earlier her sister the *Falcon* had been similarly almost lost. She had been one of the first 30-knotters to see action for, under the command of Lieutenant H. Wauton, she had been part of the escort for the battleship *Venerable* which was employed in bombarding German positions ashore on the Belgian coast. It was the duty of the Dover-based destroyers of the 6th Flotilla to provide the bombarding vessels with anti-submarine protection during these shoots and it was in performance of just such a duty that *Falcon* was engaged at midday on 28th October.

In order to reply to these attacks the Germans had installed naval batteries of heavy guns on the Flanders coast and at 1400 one of these batteries, with guns of 8-inch calibre, ranged in on the *Falcon* and hit her. The large shell exploded on the gun muzzle of one of the destroyer's little 6-pounder guns which had been replying vigorously. The effect was disastrous; the captain and seven men were killed outright while the gunner and fifteen others were wounded. Fortunately Sub-Lieutenant C. J. Du Boulay brought her to safety although a third of her crew were casualties from this one hit.

It was thought that with these old boats relegated to the more mundane chores of coastal patrol it was unlikely that they would see much surface action. In fact the 30-knotters had more action thrust upon them than many of the newer destroyers with the Grand Fleet in solitary confinement at Scapa.

The experience of the *Lively* was a case in point. She was one of the patrol destroyers based at Great Yarouth early in the war, when mines and an occasional submarine were the usual diversions. However, on the morning of the 3rd November 1914, as the flotilla steamed out to carry out their routine work, closing them at high speed was the cream of the German Navy—Admiral Hipper's Scouting Force with the battle cruisers *Seydlitz, Moltke, Blücher* and *Von der Tann*, four light cruisers with escorting torpedo-boats. They had planned to bombard Yarmouth at first light and cover a minelaying operation in the area. The fact that Great Yarmouth was normally a defenceless target was not apparently known to them.

As it was the whole squadron ran full tilt into the two leading ships of the patrol flotilla at 0705. These were two tiny vessels, the torpedo-gunboat (formerly catcher) *Halcyon* commanded by Commander G. N. Ballard, and the destroyer *Lively* commanded by Lieutenant H. T. Baillie-Grohman. *Halcyon* challenged the massive German ships and was answered by a deluge of heavy and light calibre shells which erupted all around her but which, re-markably, left her for the moment unscathed. Her end could not have been long delayed, but at this moment the *Lively* dashed up and intervened.

Courageously Baillie-Grohman took his little vessel with her 'tissue-paper' hull between the four battle-cruisers and his senior officer, laying down a well timed smoke-screen as he did so. It was the first time ever in war that a funnel smoke-screen had been laid and it worked perfectly. While *Halcyon* scurried away at her best speed the *Lively*, with the *Leopard* and *Success* coming up in support, managed to trail Hipper's giant ships and report their movements by wireless.

This remarkable and spirited action typified the instantaneous dash and bravery as well as the initiative of the young destroyer skippers, and *Lively*'s audacious foray had the result of convincing Hipper that he was possibly up against a force of which she was the mere forerunner; he turned away to carry out his bombard-ment at ten miles' range rather than the planned two. Nor did he tarry long and the effect of his heavy artillery on the towns of Yarmouth and Gorleston was minimal. The *Lively* almost cer-tainly saved a great many civilian casualties for loss of life could undoubtedly have been heavy.

Lively's escapade ended happily, but greater sacrifice was de-manded of the gallant little *Flirt*. On the night of the 26th–27th October 1916 twelve large German destroyers sortied out from Belgian ports to carry out one of their lightning raids against our Channel shipping. Dividing into two groups they steamed at high speed, half towards Boulogne, half towards Dover. Their first victim was the empty troopship *Queen* which they set on fire.

The second section of six boats was not to have it so easy, how-ever, for the Admiralty had prepared for some sort of raid by stationing several groups of destroyers across the Channel. Four lay in the Downs, five more lay at Dover with steam up in readi-ness, a further four Harwich boats were at Dunkirk also ready for action. At sea in the eastern area of the Channel was the *Flirt*, commanded by Lieutenant R. P. Kellett. Her duty was to protect an extended line of drifters on patrol against submarines.

These drifters also became the prey of the second group of German destroyers which, secure in the knowledge that any ship they encountered was hostile, pressed home their advantage. They were initially sighted by the *Flirt* who took them to be British ships returning to Dover but realised her mistake only too soon when the Germans began to roll up the line of patrol boats, sinking six drifters and damaging another four. The *Flirt* came upon the scene of carnage and began to rescue the struggling survivors, switching on her searchlight as she did so to help in this errand of mercy.

As soon as she thus revealed her position and had lowered her boat, two of the German destroyers pounced, blowing the little destroyer asunder in minutes. She sank with all hands, the only survivors being the boat's crew away hunting for survivors. The lessons of war were hard to accept for the Royal Navy and the natural inclination of rescue and succour for the victims of attacks and sinkings led to repeated casualties before it sank home that the Germans were fighting a very different kind of war. Here, despite the tragic example of the *Hogue*, *Crecy* and *Aboukir* earlier in the war, Lieutenant Kellett's first action had been to save the survivors and he and his ship's company paid the price.

Those 30-knotters which came through the war unscathed were naturally very quickly sold off for scrap in 1919 and by the following year they had all gone. They had laid the foundations of the destroyer service and, together with the 27-knotters, had shown that the high speeds required were attainable but at a price. Although the little turtle-back boats were soon to take a back seat in destroyer development, nearly every destroyer officer of the First World War gained some experience with them. They were the last individual boats of the destroyer story, every one was unique, their names were the perfect match of the speed, agility and grace of which they could boast. *Flirt, Flying Fish, Cheerful* and *Foam*: quaint these names may sound today, but a study of the ships which bore them makes all the more regrettable the later adoption of the featureless standardised 'Battle', 'Weapon' and 'Hunt' groupings in the years which followed.

Chapter V

Tragedies and Caution

Although the French *Forban* gained world-wide fame by exceeding 31 knots in September 1895 it was the outstanding performance of the *Hai Lung*, a Chinese destroyer built by Schichau of Elbing, which caused the most worry in naval circles. This boat was reputed to have attained the stunning speed of 31·1 knots over the measured mile. Although France was still our potential enemy, no one could deny the rapid growth, power and influence of the new German Empire. Particularly outstanding was the growth of their Navy and it soon became clear that the resources of that dynamic nation were more than sufficient to gain equality in numbers; given the time, they could also show a marked superiority in many facets of warship construction.

It was thought highly desirable that the Royal Navy should have destroyers which could at least match this performance, but unfortunately the development limits of the reciprocating engine had been just about reached. In order to achieve new records the boats grew larger, although, as pointed out earlier, at a certain point this increase in displacement offsets any gain in engine power and becomes self-defeating. The turbine engine was just around the corner and was to provide the answer, but in 1896 the Admiralty placed orders for several 'Special' destroyers with skilled builders, which were still to be equipped with reciprocating engines in a final attempt to achieve the ultimate in speed as envisaged at that time.

The Thornycroft-built *Albatross* (see Table 4) was designed for 32 knots and was much larger than the 30-knotters already on the stocks, displacing 430 tons. Launched in July 1898 at a total cost of £66,500 she carried out a prolonged period of trials but failed to reach the figure striven for. Although she developed 7,732 hp on test, a figure which *exceeded* that of her design (7,500 hp) she nevertheless only achieved a maximum speed of 31·35 knots and on this she was accepted.

The Laird Brothers' 'Special', the *Express* (see Table 6), turned out to be larger still and was the first to be completed ready for trial. She was not to be first to sea, however, for no less than sixteen sets of propellers were tried out in an effort to reach 32 knots. The first trial did in fact produce one run of 32 knots but the mean was 30.9. With her engines developing a then record 9,882 hp, something more than this was expected and the Admiralty obviously wanted something more than this for the total £62,500 she cost—over £10,000 more than the average 30-knotter.

Unfortunately the *Express* appeared to be a jinx ship and during her seventeen months of trials she never exceeded 32 knots. Further, she was damaged in dock during this period which further delayed her completion. At last an exasperated Admiralty accepted her, but insisted on the full penalties being paid. Further trials were beset by difficulties and finally after completing twenty-seven preliminary and thirteen official trials *Express* entered service in 1900. Even so she was never a successful ship and continually broke down at high speed, although she somehow remained in service throughout the Great War.

The last of this trio of unfortunate vessels was the *Arab*, another large destroyer of some 470 tons, at that time the heaviest displacement among torpedo craft. She was constructed by Thomson and fitted with Normand boilers. Laid down later than the others she was not launched until 1901 by which time she had been overtaken by events and was left rather an odd ship out. This sad state of affairs was not improved by the fact that she also failed to reach her contract speed, turning in a poor 30·5 knots as her best performance. Again the penalty was exacted by the Admiralty, £3,000, which finished Thomson's interest in this specialised area of ship construction. The *Arab* joined the fleet late in 1901.

It was obvious from the performance of these three vessels that something new was required to achieve the sought-for breakthrough and by a happy chance this was provided at the Naval Review at Spithead in 1897.

The arrival of the turbine happily coincided with the final development of the reciprocating engine, the early experiments of De Laval being perfected for maritime use by Charles Parsons. In the simplest terms, a system of curved blades are fixed in grooves along a shaft, at certain angles, and projecting radially outward.

The surrounding casing has corresponding blades fitted inside and steam from the boilers is directed on to these fixed blades which deflect it to the moving blades on the shaft. This in turn rotates a drum fixed to the shaft driving the propellers.

The advantages of small size, few working parts and smoother running soon became obvious, and although the adoption of the turbine was delayed, this was through no fault of the turbine itself. A disadvantage, which was more than offset by the improvements, was the fact that at reduced speed there was a considerable falling off of efficiency and because of this additional 'cruising' turbines had to be carried.

The advent of the steam turbine was marked by a dramatic piece of showmanship from Charles Parsons, who had been experimenting with them since the 1880s with growing success. The idea itself was far from a new one, but Parsons it was who succeeded in utilising it in a practical fashion suitable for ship propulsion. By 1897 he had constructed the little *Turbinia* and tests were conducted to the satisfaction of the DNC.

At the Diamond Jubilee Naval Review, Parsons took his little craft in among the lines of anchored warships to demonstrate her speed and power. To the astonishment of most of those who witnessed her performance, she touched speeds of 35 knots and was the outstanding attraction of the Review.

Following a proposal by Parsons, the Admiralty decided to contract for a turbine-driven destroyer; the hull was sub-contracted out to Hawthorn Leslie, while Yarrow boilers were employed. This vessel, the *Viper*, was launched in September 1899. Her turbines developed 10,000 hp for the required 32 knots and she easily outpaced this by achieving a staggering 36·5 knots over a six-run trial, with a maximum of 37·118. True she ran her trials light in the usual custom, but even so this was remarkable. She was free from vibration as compared with normally engined boats and economical in that she had a fuel consumption of only 2·38 pounds per iph/hours at 31 knots. (Compare with earlier boats, see page 55).

She was a handsome looking vessel of 344 tons displacement with three big squat funnels and enormous ventilating cowls between them, with the usual 30-knotter hull form and turtle-back. She continued to achieve impressive and fast speeds, but it was found that at low speeds coal consumption went up when compared with the average destroyer. She certainly had tremendous impact on destroyer design when the figures of her trials became known.

A second destroyer fitted with Mr Parsons's remarkable engines soon joined the *Viper* on test. This was the *Cobra* constructed by Armstrongs at Elswick as a 'stock' destroyer and launched in June 1899. Stock ships were vessels laid down as speculations and offered to the Admiralty or other suitable customers when completed. This particular vessel was damaged in a collision soon after completing and it was not until she had been repaired that she was put on offer. The Admiralty inspected her and found her structurally weak. After some strengthening had been worked in they bought her for £63,500 for use as a second test-bed for the turbine.

By June 1901 she was ready for trial and the *Cobra*, with the same dimensions and power as the *Viper*, turned in a mean speed of 34·7 knots with a maximum of 35·6. As with the *Viper*, it was found that an enormous increase in the numbers of engine room staff was required to keep her insatiable boilers supplied. In fact the First Lord baulked at the prospect of having a fleet composed of similar vessels, despite their phenomenal speeds, precisely because of the increase in the stoker complement required:

> It is contrary to all sense of fitness to have 80 men in a destroyer. It is preferable to sacrifice speed rather than suffer this undesirably large complement.

Despite this the turbine had apparently proven itself, being easily able to exceed the required contract speeds.

Unfortunately soon after their initial successes both these destroyers came to tragic ends. The *Viper* under the command of Lieutenant Speke was included in the 1901 Manoeuvres and was despatched from Portsmouth on the afternoon of the 3rd August to search for 'enemy' torpedo-boats off the Channel Islands. The weather deteriorated and speed was reduced from 22 to 16 knots. Dense fog descended but on sighting Torpedo-boat 81, one of the 'hostile' force, the *Viper* speeded up to avoid her, again at 22 knots. At 5.25 pm she struck the Reconquet reef tearing out her bottom. The torpedo-boat followed her aground and both were total losses. The wreck lay on the Casquets at Alderney but soon broke up; the remains were sold for scrap. Lieutenant Speke was reprimanded, but fortunately there had been no loss of life.

Five weeks later the *Cobra* was adjudged ready for delivery and a naval party commanded by Lieutenant Bosworth Smith went aboard her to take her down the coast to Portsmouth. Also aboard were representatives of the builders and the Parsons Company, including the manager, Mr Barnard. On the way south heavy weather was encountered off Flamborough Head and the *Cobra* began rolling severely; so bad in fact was her motion that speed was reduced down to 10 knots and difficulty was encountered in manning the stokeholds at all.

At 0700, a bare two hours after sailing, the *Cobra* buckled up, broke her back and foundered in sight of the Outer Dowsing Lightship. Apparently her back had broken across between the two after boilers, her stern section sinking right away. The wreckage of her fore section was later found upside down on the bottom. Only twelve men were rescued from all those on board—a crippling blow to Parsons who had sent some of their most skilled men on the trip.

The public outcry forced a Court of Enquiry and tests made with the *Wolf* led to the conclusion that the *Cobra* was structurally unsound when she put to sea; the court also decided that the turbines were in no way responsible, but despite this, with the loss of two destroyers within six weeks of each other, there was an obvious reaction against these engines. There was also a reaction against the use of snake names in the Service after this.

Although the Parsons engines were in no way to blame for these disasters, there was a considerable slowing-down on their subsequent development as a result. It was thought that too much was being asked of the little ships—and, indeed, on a 350-ton displacement it probably was. Be that as it may, the Admiralty decided on a policy of caution and only one further vessel was put in hand for leisurely experiments.

This boat was the *Velox*, built by Hawthorn Leslie and equipped with a modified set of Parsons turbines in an effort to reduce the low-speed coal consumption which had so bedevilled the earlier two vessels. After considerable argument the Admiralty purchased her for £67,000 but only after they had insisted upon many alterations.

Trials began in 1902. She was of the same dimensions as the *Viper* and had four shafts and eight propellers with high pressure on the outer, and low on the inner, shafts. In addition she had two small auxiliary triple expansion engines for cruising. One feature of her initial trials was the excessive noise of the stokehold fans. She was a handsome vessel, but an inbuilt fault which marred her subsequent life was that her condensers were above the waterline and this frequently led to engine breakdowns in heavy seas, due to loss of suction.

She was by no means as sensational on her trials as the *Viper*; indeed, although she achieved one good run of 33·64 knots on a preliminary attempt, she was never able to make much more than 28 knots on any subsequent occasion. Nor was she an economical steamer. By 1909 reports from sea were so generally unfavourable that she was sent into Portsmouth in disgrace, being attached permanently to HMS *Vernon* as 'no longer regarded as fit for sea services'. There she had to spend her days, surviving through to the war, and from there she was mined off the Nab Lightship on 25th October 1915.

The overall results from both the turbine and conventional experimental boats had been extremely discouraging and a reversion was made to a type which was more seaworthy and sturdy, but in which speed came a poor second to endurance. The only other classic turtle-back destroyers which entered the Navy were the two stock destroyers built by Parsons in 1906. Fitted with turbines, they looked out of place against the new 'River' Class boats. The Parsons boats' best speeds were 26 knots and they survived to serve through the war, being broken up in 1919.

In addition to the reaction against high speeds there was another important factor which weighed heavily with the Admiralty when it came to considering the design of the next class of destroyers, the 'River' Class. This was their range. In 1901 there was set up a 'Committee on TBD'. Among the many points discussed was a long list of superior points noted in the German destroyers over our own and made during a visit to Wilhelmshaven and Kiel that summer.

Schichau's 'S.90' Class had a radius of action of 3,150 nautical miles and showed other such outstanding features as a good bridge positioned well above the waterline, high bows and fo'c'sle with a gap to allow the breaking water to avoid the bridge and charthouse, and far superior accommodation. Displacing some 400 tons they set the pattern for future German destroyer construction in that they mounted torpedo tubes in the bridge-well designed to fire ahead. The Germans also restricted their large destroyer building programme to three builders only who specialised in these craft which gave their flotillas a degree of uniformity never attained by the British boats of the 'nineties'. The Germans never referred to their ships as 'destroyers', retaining the old term 'torpedo-boat' throughout, although their ships would have rated as destroyers in any other navy in the world; a precise reason for this is not known.

As well as taking note of these advantages in the German boats, it was also decided that, instead of the largely fictitious speed attributed to TBDs in the past, the new British boats must carry out their trials at deep load draught, the requirement in this trim being a speed of 25·5 knots, which would be more of a true speed for comparison. Unfortunately, this was not generally realised by the public and there was some outcry when the trial speeds for the next destroyers were announced.

With an average displacement of 550 tons and with the soon-to-be-traditional high raised fo'c'sle, the 'Rivers' set the pace and style for almost all subsequent British destroyer design. High-tensile steel was used extensively and galvanisation was also carried out on the upper deck plating. Besides improving seaworthiness, the high fo'c'sle gave vastly improved accommodation for the men and each officer now had a separate cabin, an unheard-of luxury in TBDs and one which finished the 'Hard Lying' conditions* for ever! Complement was sixty-four officers and men, but the armament was disappointing, being the standard single 12-pounder, five 6-pounders and two torpedo tubes, the same as in the much smaller 30-knotters. This arrangement was of short duration and reports from observers of the Russo-Japanese War soon persuaded the Admiralty to fit the larger 12-pounder gun throughout as it was now recognised that the 6-pounder was useless in stopping torpedo craft. They carried a whaler and a dinghy, both on davits, in addition to the usual Berthon.

As before, with half a dozen builders the ships did not present a uniform outline but retained in batches their constructor's own peculiar interpretations of the Admiralty's specification. All were fitted with triple-expansion engines developing around 7,300 ihp

* Payment of 'Hard Lying' money continued until the 1920's, and was revived for some boats during World War II.

with the sole exception of the *Eden* which was fitted with turbines. All made their contract speeds, but few exceeded it by any great margin. *Eden* with her Parsons came out the fastest at 26·2 knots but the difficulties of economy at normal speeds persisted, the 14 knots given by her cruising auxiliaries being too low for usual flotilla requirements. Exhaustive comparison tests with the *Derwent* merely confirmed this fact.

But there was no denying the superior sea-keeping qualities of the class, their raised fo'c'sle reaping dividends and making life aboard a TBD bearable for the first time. Report after report emphasised the excellence of this feature, although when the first 'Rivers' appeared at sea, the general opinion was far from enthusiastic. *The Times* Correspondent of 1904 was scathing:

The latest destroyers in their dimensions closely approach the torpedo-gunboats of the 'Sharpshooter' class. They are somewhat similar in displacement, much inferior in weight of armament and have much smaller boiler capacity and power of covering distance; but they are considerably faster, and cost much more than the 'Sharpshooter'. The new type destroyer is about 75 per cent greater in displacement than the 30-knotter destroyers and cost is about 25 per cent greater. Sea keeping capability has been increased somewhat, no doubt, by increased dimensions and by the construction of high forecastles similar to those adopted 17 years ago in the 'Sharpshooter' class.

He continued in much the same vein that neither in size, nor in coal capacity, nor in maintaining speed in rough water, could the 'Rivers' be regarded as independent sea commands, or scouts, while in the primary purpose of the destroyer itself their low speed made them distinctly inferior to the 30-knotter type. He added that it should not be forgotten that the latest sea-going torpedo-boats of our own and foreign navies had attained speeds of 25 to 26 knots in smooth water and that some were faster in smooth water than our present 30-knotters.

Nor was *The Times* alone in its criticism, for the Commander in Chief of the Channel Fleet, Vice Admiral Lord Charles Beresford, composed a detailed list of the disadvantages of the 'Rivers' over the previous TBDs. His main points were that much higher costs per ship and increased complements were not offset by the greater seaworthiness because 'the 30-knotters can keep their speed in any weather in which a torpedo boat can keep its speed and cost

£15,000 to £20,000 less, so it would appear more can be had for the same money, in the proportion of three to two'.

But the Manoeuvres of 1904 finally gave convincing proof of the superiority of the 'Rivers'. They kept their speed when the older boats had to return to harbour, their 12-pounders could still be fired and conditions aboard were vastly superior at all times. The most discussed incident in their favour was the cruise to Singapore undertaken by six of the 'Rivers' in 1905, which proved their economy. The *Dee* and the *Exe* left Singapore for Hong Kong and ran full into a typhoon en route with no way of avoiding it; they had to pass right through its centre. Both vessels received a severe hammering—at times 'the keel of *Dee* was visible to the foremost funnel'—and they both suffered flooding and damage to upperworks but their engines and boilers were unharmed and they came through this unique experienced comparatively unscathed for vessels of their size.

Considerable interest was naturally taken in the Russo-Japanese War which was in process in the Far East at the time; and this war afforded the first real test for the destroyers, as it did indeed for all the modern types of naval ordnance and warships developed over the previous century. Again British observers reported at length and drew conclusions from every action. The torpedo featured in most of the Japanese successes, but all in all its total effect in comparison with the results expected of it were meagre.

For example, during the initial attack on the Russian Squadron at Port Arthur on 8th February the Japanese employed five divisions of destroyers totalling some eighteen boats and, as was later recorded, no torpedo attack could have been delivered in conditions more favourable to the weapon. The enemy was in an exposed position, had taken no special precautions against an attack, and indeed was not expecting one. His whereabouts were accurately known, thus eliminating any need to scout in advance. The weather was perfect with no moon. But despite all this, no Russian ship was actually sunk, although three were damaged. Some of the Japanese torpedoes did not even detonate.

A further example of the apparent unreliability of the torpedo as a weapon of war was given in the follow-up attack on 13th February. A destroyer flotilla sortied against Port Arthur through a thick snowstorm. Despite the 'incomparable skill' with which

75

the Japanese skippers handled their craft, the attack failed completely.

However indifferently the torpedo itself behaved, though, there was no doubt as to the performance of the British-built and designed destroyers. Admiral Togo himself testified that:

> Destroyers built in Britain by Messrs Yarrow and Thornycroft for the Japanese Navy have been continually and successfully employed in wild winter weather under the trying conditions prevailing during operations against Port Arthur. Although severely tried there is no weakness in hull or machinery.

The Admiralty were quite satisfied with the 'Rivers' and for the 1904–5 programme the type was to be modified but basically continued in its present form. However, with the arrival of Admiral Sir John Fisher at the Admiralty as First Sea Lord these plans were instantly dismissed. 'Jackie' Fisher had ideas of his own!

The officer complement of a 'River' around 1907 would have consisted of a lieutenant as commanding officer (the term lieutenant-commander was not adopted until the outbreak of the war—up to that time the correct title was lieutenant-in-command); the first lieutenant would be in actual fact a sub lieutenant; while Lionel Dawson recalled that the gunner

> . . . seemed invariably to be 'just made' from the lower deck, or about to depart on pension; while the engineer officer was usually senior in service to his captain.

The last reciprocating-engined destroyers, the 'Rivers', saw much strenuous service in peace and war. A few firms built stock destroyers to the general 'River' design and these were later bought in by the Admiralty to replace losses, which proved to be heavy. These were the *Rother* built by Palmers in 1903, and the *Test* and *Stour* built by Cammell Laird in 1909 and only purchased because of their cheapness! Other firms with unasked-for 'Rivers' complete were left with them; they had to scrap them on the slipways with resultant losses, as Fisher had no interest in them. Speed was his obsession, and so the pendulum swung back again.

In service the 'Rivers' gave good value for money. They were also kept busy. During manoeuvres near the Outer Gabbard Light Vessel on 27th April 1908 the scout *Attentive* sliced the *Gala* in half and damaged the *Welland* in a night collision with resultant casualties. The *Blackwater* went down off Dungeness after being hit by a merchant ship on 6th April the following year. The *Wear* was damaged in a similar incident on 13th January 1907 near the Royal Sovereign Lightship. This was the period of 'realistic' manoeuvres during which the TBDs were driven very hard—and they proved very costly in ships and lives. Both *Eden* and *Ness* went aground in 1910 but were subsequently repaired.

*   *   *   *   *

On the outbreak of war many of the 'Rivers' were with the Dover Patrol, while the China boats found themselves acting as mine-sweepers during the Dardenelles Campaign; the *Chelmer, Colne, Garry, Ribble, Usk* and *Wear* all served in the Dardanelles. Several of them performed gallant work when the old battleships employed in the bombardments began to suffer losses from mining, which their ancient hulls were not built to withstand.

On 8th March the French battleship *Bouvet* struck a mine off Gallipoli which exploded her magazine; she blew up and sank in under two minutes. Despite the suddenness of her passing, the *Wear* (Captain C. P. Metcalfe) which had been standing by the *Queen Elizabeth* was quickly on the scene and managed to pick up sixty-six men with her whaler, although under fire from the Turkish batteries ashore. This took place at 1400 hours. Some four and a quarter hours later the old *Irresistible* also came to grief and *Wear* was once again quickly in the picture, running alongside the heeling vessel. Within the space of half an hour she had embarked no less than twenty-eight officers and 582 men.

Meanwhile the French *Gaulois* had received heavy damage from shell fire and steamed slowly out of action with her fo'c'sle awash. It was thought advisable to take off some of her crew in case she foundered and the *Chelmer* (Lieutenant-Commander H. T. England) went alongside her and embarked 400 men which she transferred to the *Dartmouth*.

Disaster followed disaster as the battleship force blundered over the unsuspected minefield. The battle-cruiser *Inflexible* struck one and was damaged though fortunately she remained afloat, and then the *Ocean* struck another and was severely damaged. With the *Wear* (and two 'Beagle' Class boats) the *Colne* (Commander C. Seymour), *Chelmer, Jed* (Lieutenant G. F. A. Mulock) and *Kennet*

77

(Lieutenant C. E. S. Farrant) went to her aid. The Turks laid down a very heavy fire on this mercy mission and the group was surrounded by shell splashes. The *Racoon* was damaged by the concussion of an under-water shell-burst, but all ships survived though suffering casualties.

Chelmer embarked about 500 of the crew of the *Ocean*—after the latter had assumed a 15-degree list—and on one occasion was lifted bodily out of the water by the explosion of a mine or salvo which only just missed her. Eighteen feet of *Chelmer*'s bottom were blown in and the centre boiler-room was flooded, but she carried on her rescue work. She completed temporary repairs alongside the Depot Ship *Blenheim* and was back at work within a brief period.

Such heavy losses led to the abandonment of the purely naval attack and plans were made to land troops. And so the Gallipoli Campaign began, only to end in yet another murderous slogging match, in which the Allies exchanged tens of thousands of lives for a few hundred yards of mud and wire. The destroyers had an eventful time in support of the operations ashore but were spared its ghastly carnage. For the landings at Anzac Cove the destroyers were employed in carrying troops and towing the landing boats into position: *Chelmer, Usk* (Lieutenant-Commander W. G. C. Maxwell) and *Ribble* (Lieutenant-Commander R. W. Wilkinson) were all thus employed.

Chelmer was again in action when the Battleship *Triumph* was torpedoed. Although *Triumph* was steaming in circles with her torpedo nets out a German submarine commander evaded the escorting destroyer and his torpedo slammed straight through the nets as if they had not been there. *Chelmer* went alongside—and remained there for twenty minutes with the old battleship threatening to capsize on top of her—and embarked nearly all *Triumph*'s crew. The submarine escaped unscathed.

Various small operations relieved the tedium of normal duties of patrol and close support, the *Jed* landing a party for a raid in the Gulf of Xeros, while the *Kennet* assisted in a raid on Budrum, a Turkish port in the Gulf of Cos thought to be the base for the prowling U-boats who were inflicting so much damage in the Dardenelles. *Chelmer* and *Colne* were much in evidence providing support fire at Anzac and *Chelmer* wore out her 12-cwt 12-pounder firing 1,375 rounds, while her other mountings became so worn that they acted like howitzers—which the naval gunners found excellent for bombarding the Turkish trenches.

Nearer home, the *Garry* (Commander W. W. Wilson) carried out a successful ramming of the *U.18* off Scapa Flow on 23rd November 1914 which resulted in the submarine being scuttled by her crew. The *Garry* picked up all the crew save one. The *Ouse* was credited with two sinkings in 1918. Further afield, *Ribble, Usk* and *Welland* had earlier assisted in the capture of Tsing-tao by the Japanese in 1914 before proceeding to the Mediterranean.

Losses were heavy; three 'Rivers' were mined, the *Foyle* in the Dover Straits on 15th March 1917, the *Derwent* off Le Havre on 2nd May the same year and *Kale* in the North Sea on the 27th March 1918. Other losses were the *Erne*, which was wrecked off Rattray Head on 6th February 1915, and the *Eden*, which was lost after a collision in the Channel, 18th June 1916. The final casualty, the *Itchen*, was torpedoed and sunk in the North Sea on 6th July 1917 by a U-boat.

After the war was over, the others, well past their age-limit, went quickly to the scrapyards in the years 1919 and 1920.

Chapter VI

Fisher's Boats

In 1905, when the 'Rivers' were still joining the fleet, there was much haziness with regard to the correct employment of the destroyers within the modern fleet and the eye witness reports of the Russo-Japanese conflict had done little to clarify the problem. While it was obvious that their original task of destroying hostile torpedo-boats still held good, the growing size of the destroyer opened up new horizons. Vice-Admiral Sir Baldwin Walker had given the subject considerable thought and he set forth his views in a book published at that time. He listed the four main functions of the TBDs which were summarised as:

1. Screening the advance of a fleet when hostile torpedo craft are about.
2. Searching a hostile coast along which a fleet must pass.
3. Watching an enemy's port for the purpose of harassing his torpedo craft when leaving and preventing their return.
4. Attacking an enemy's fleet.

To perform 1 and 4 the destroyers must obviously be larger and able to maintain the course and speed of the main fleets, while for 2 and 3 smaller vessels were quite adequate. Admiral Walker dismissed the idea of using destroyers in the scout or cruiser role for—owing to their size and the cramped conditions of their bridges—visibility was poor, positioning uncertain and officers few. Nevertheless, when Fisher arrived in Whitehall his intention was the abolition of the small cruiser and its replacement with large destroyers fitted with wireless. These would act as a scouting screen to cover the enemy's harbours and give warning to the main fleets when the enemy ventured to sea.

Fisher never had any time for small destroyers, but despite this the Committee of Designs he set up was given its briefing which stated flatly that the Board of Admiralty had decided on two types of Torpedo Craft in lieu of the proposed 'Improved Rivers'. The

Turbinia steaming at 34¾ knots on her turbines

18. *Turbinia* at the Spithead Naval Review of 1897 where her high speed caused a sensation

19. A mixed bag of destroyers—the picture gives some idea of the complexity of design which could confront a flotilla commander.

TABLE 6: Special Destroyers

Armament for all the 'Specials' was the same as the 30-Knotters: one 12-pounder; five 6-pounders; and two 18-inch torpedo-tubes.

Albacore and *Bonetta*: in 1906 Palmers launched two stock destroyers and these were purchased by the Admiralty on completion in 1909 to replace *Lee* and *Tiger* which had been lost; Parsons turbines were fitted to both. Speed: *Albacore* 26·8; *Bonetta* 26·7.

Name	Builder	Tonnage	Dimensions
Albacore	Palmers	440	215½ × 21
Bonetta	Palmers	440	215½ × 21

Ultimate disposal: both ships were broken up 1919–21.

Arab: built by Clydebank and fitted with Normand boilers as a reply to the French *Forban* of 1895; the order was placed in 1896 with Thomsons and completed in 1901 by John Brown, but her best speed was only 30·5 knots and she cost £63,640 after payment of penalties.

Name	Builder	Tonnage	Dimensions
Arab	Thomsons	470	227½ × 23¼

Ultimate disposal: broken up in 1919–21.

Express: laid down with *Arab* and *Albatross* (see Table 4) to match French *Forban* and German *Hai Lung* designs, she proved of unfortunate design and was only finally accepted into service after running no less than 27 preliminary and 13 official trials; she only reached the modest speed of 31·6 knots despite extra power; her cost was £62,500.

Name	Builder	Tonnage	Dimensions
Express	Laird	465	235¼ × 23½

Ultimate disposal: sold in 1921.

Three experimental turbine boats laid down after the *Turbinia* had opened the Admiralty's eyes at Spithead in 1897. The first of these, *Viper*, was ordered from the Parsons Steam Turbine Company who sub-contracted the hull to Hawthorn Leslie; she cost £53,000 and achieved a speed of 36·6. The second turbine boat, *Cobra*, was built by Armstrongs and launched in 1899. She undertook numerous trials and was lost on passage for delivery. She cost £63,500 and achieved a speed of 30·1. The third boat, *Velox*, though more fortunate than her two predecessors, proved very unsuccessful on trials and was not popular in service; she cost £67,275 and gave a speed of 27·75.

Name	Builder	Tonnage	Dimensions
Viper	Parsons Leslie	344	210¼ × 21
Cobra	Armstrong	375	223½ × 20¼
Velox	Parsons Leslie	462	210 × 21

Ultimate disposal: *Viper* was wrecked on the Reconquet Reef off Alderney in 1901; *Cobra* foundered in heavy seas the same year; *Velox* was sunk by a mine in 1915.

21. The 'Stock Destroyer' *Bonetta*, built by Palmer and bought by the Royal Navy in 1909

22. The ill-fated *Cobra*, built by Armstrongs—she foundered in heavy seas on her first voyage

23. *Usk*, built by Yarrow in 1903

distinctive paired smoke-stacks

24. *Itchen*, from Cammell Laird in 1903, showing her clean lines. The 12-pounder is raised on the fo'c's'le and she has two 6-pounders in the waist at the break in the fo'c's'le

25 The Palmer-built *Rother* in 1909 with close-paired funnels

TABLE 7: The 'River' Class

Thirty-six ships, completed in 1903–6, at an average cost of £70,000. Armament: one 12-pounder; five 6-pounders; and two 18-inch torpedo-tubes. The gun armament was later altered to four 12-pounders. Speed: best *Eden* and *Gala* 26·2; worst *Cherwell* and *Teviot* 25·2.

Name	Builder	Tonnage	Dimensions
Arun	Laird	550	220 × 23¾
Blackwater	Laird	550	220 × 23¾
Boyne	Hawthorn Leslie	545	220 × 23½
Chelmer	Thornycroft	560	222 × 23¾
Cherwell	Palmer	549	225 × 23½
Colne	Thornycroft	560	222 × 23¾
Dee	Palmer	545	225 × 23½
Derwent	Hawthorn Leslie	540	220 × 23½
Doon	Hawthorn Leslie	545	220 × 23½
Eden	Hawthorn Leslie	540	220 × 23½
Erne	Palmer	545	225 × 23¾
Ettrick	Palmer	545	225 × 23¾
Exe	Palmer	545	225 × 23¾
Foyle	Laird Brothers	549	220 × 23¾
Gala	Yarrow	570	225 × 23½
Garry	Yarrow	570	225 × 23½
Itchen	Laird	550	220 × 23¾
Jed	Thornycroft	550	220 × 23½
Kale	Hawthorn Leslie	545	220 × 23½
Kennet	Thornycroft	550	220 × 23¾
Liffey	Laird	550	220 × 23¾
Moy	Laird	550	220 × 23¾
Ness	White	555	224½ × 23¾
Nith	White	555	224½ × 23¾
Ouse	Laird	550	220 × 23¾
Ribble	Yarrow	570	225 × 23½
Rother	Palmer	545	225 × 23¾
Stour	Cammell Laird	570	220 × 23¾
Swale	Palmer	545	225 × 23¾
Test	Cammell Laird	570	225 × 23¾
Teviot	Yarrow	555	225 × 23½
Ure	Palmer	550	225 × 23¾
Usk	Yarrow	555	225 × 23½
Waveney	Hawthorn Leslie	552	220 × 23½
Wear	Palmer	550	225 × 23¾
Welland	Yarrow	555	225 × 23½

Ultimate disposal: *Gala* was sliced in half by *Attentive* off Harwich in 1908; *Blackwater* was sunk in collision off Dungeness in 1909; *Erne* was wrecked off Rattray Head, 1915; *Eden* was sunk in a collision in the Channel in 1916; *Derwent* was mined in 1916; *Foyle* and *Kale* likewise in 1917 and 1918; *Itchen* was torpedoed by a U-boat in the North Sea in 1917; all the others were sold and scrapped 1919–20.

TABLE 8: The 'Ocean' Class

Twelve ships, completed in 1907–9 at an average cost of £135,400. Armament: the first five had three 12-pounders—later four 12-pounders; and two 18-inch torpedo-tubes; the remainder had two 4-inch guns, and two 18-inch torpedo-tubes. Speed: best *Tartar* 35·3; worst *Saracen* 33·1.

Name	Builder	Tonnage	Dimensions
Afridi	Armstrongs	855	250 × 24½
Amazon	Thornycroft	970	280¼ × 26¼
Cossack	Cammell Laird	882	270 × 26
Crusader	White	1045	280 × 26
Ghurka	Hawthorn Leslie	872	255 × 25½
Maori	Denny	1026	280 × 27
Mohawk	White	864	270 × 25
Nubian	Thornycroft	998	280 × 26¾
Saracen	White	980	272 × 26
Tartar	Thornycroft	850	270 × 26
Viking	Palmer	1090	280 × 27½
Zulu	Hawthorn Leslie	1027	280 × 27

Ultimate disposal: *Nubian* was torpedoed in October 1916 and *Zulu* was mined in November 1916; both were used to construct the composite *Zubian* which was sold in 1919; *Ghurka* was mined, February 1917; all the others were sold and scrapped 1919–20.

'Special'

One large experimental boat was built to Fisher's design specification; originally named *Flying Scud*, she cost £236,000. Her armament was four 4-inch guns, one 2-pounder and two 18-inch torpedo-tubes. Her speed was 35·03 knots.

Name	Builder	Tonnage	Dimensions
Swift	Cammell Laird	2170	345 × 34

Ultimate disposal: after much hard service she was scrapped in 1921.

27. *Viking*, built by Palmer in 1909—the only six-funnelled ship built for the Royal Navy

28. *Tartar*, from Thornycroft, in 1907, which can be compared with *Nubian* from the same firm, Plate 29

first were described as Ocean-going Destroyers of about 600 tons, armed with three 12-pounders and two torpedo-tubes. Speed of the order of 33 to 34 knots was required, seagoing, for eight hours. The second group were described as Coastal Service Destroyers with dimensions similar to the original 27-knotters, 250 tons, with an armament of two 12-pounders and three torpedo-tubes, with seagoing speed of 26 knots like the 'Rivers'. In addition, a super-fast design was called for by Fisher from which operational speeds of *36* knots were demanded!

Seven specialist firms were asked to tender for the first five 'Oceans'—as the larger destroyers were called—the specification being as above; the firms were allowed a completely free hand but only given eleven days in which to reply with the tender and design.

The 'Coastal' Class of destroyer eventually turned out to be the 'Insect' Class, ships of around 250 tons of which no less than thirty-six were completed in the years 1906–9. The latter boats contained many refinements and were fitted with the new steam capstans. All were fitted with turbines and performed ably enough in the role intended for them, but it was soon decided that they were too frail to be distinguished as destroyers at all; their names were dropped and they were re-rated First-Class Torpedo-Boats and given numbers 1–36. In the service they were very popular commands for young officers and were affectionately known as 'Oily Wads'.

When the tenders for the 'Oceans' came back the lowest was from Yarrow, £95,000, the highest from Palmers,£137,500. Such figures gave the Admiralty a heart attack and the firms were told to think again. Finally contracts were awarded to Elswick, Laird, Hawthorn, White and Thornycroft. Yarrows, who had put in the lowest tender, were rejected in favour of Elswick whose only experience in the destroyer field was the *Cobra*!

That the Director of Naval Construction, the then Mr Philip Watts [Oscar Parkes wrote], had lately returned to the Admiralty from Elswick was doubtless a coincidence of influence.

No ship was in any way similar and the 'Oceans' must be described as a series of individual ships rather than as a class. Penalties imposed were exacting: £10,000 per knot below the contract speed; but as a substantial spur the bonus per knot was of an equal amount.

These large vessels were given stirring names, many of them of famous fighting tribes of the Empire, and they soon became popularly known as the 'Tribals' and as such we shall refer to them here.

First launched was Lairds' *Cossack*. She was of 855 tons displacement, 270 feet long and cost £140,935. She was fitted with five of Lairds' own design boilers and on her trial attained a mean of 34 knots, with 14,000 horsepower. Extensive trials were conducted to try and ascertain the influence of the depth of water on speed, the deep water Skelmorlie being known to give slower speeds for the same vessel than the Maplin course. Lairds received £1,000 bonus for her speed, but over half this was deducted as she was delivered almost a year late. She had a raised 'River'-type fo'c'sle, as did the *Afridi* and *Ghurka*. The *Mohawk* had a slight turtle deck and the *Tartar* was different again in having a high sheer—an outward-curving, flowing hull-line at her bows—and turtle deck with the forward 12-pounders on a raised platform. Both these latter ships were later rebuilt with conventional fo'c'sles.

Afridi, the Elswick boat, was the smallest of the batch and also turned out the slowest. She was three-quarters of a knot below the contract speed at Maplin and only got by four months later, after repeated trials, by the barest edge. The DNC pleaded the experimental nature of the work and Elswick's were not penalised. She was twenty-six months late on delivery when she was finally accepted in September 1909. Both *Afridi* and *Cossack* had three squat funnels.

The *Ghurka*, built by Hawthorns, came out at 885 tons and was boilered with five Yarrow water-tubes; she achieved a trial mean of 33·9 with 14,240 ihp. A maximum of $36\frac{1}{2}$ knots was achieved on her fastest run at St Abbs Head, and Hawthorns got their £10,000 bonus. She turned out an excellent sea-boat.

The *Mohawk*, from Whites, was of 865 tons, 270 feet long, with six White-Forster boilers developing 14,500 ihp. She ran her trials over the shallow Maplin course and turned in 34·25 knots which was sufficient to gain her builders the due bonus payment. Her turtle-back fo'c'sle turned out to be a poor investment and tended to make her wet in service. Like most of these vessels, and many others of the Fisher era, the *Mohawk* had to have her foremost funnel raised to ease the problem of hot gases, smoke and heat over her bridge.

Fastest of the initial batch was Thornycroft's *Tartar*. Displacing 945 tons, an enormous tonnage for a destroyer of that time, she developed 14,500 ihp with six Thornycroft boilers. On the Maplin she did 35·36 knots, a very satisfactory performance, and her builders received £12,000. By contrast the Admiralty refused to award any amount to Whites although their vessel had exceeded the contract speed over the same course.

When the case eventually came to court the Admiralty, through their Chief Constructor W. H. Whiting, insisted that the special benefits of the Maplin Mile for vessels of over 25 knots were worth an extra knot; and so they claimed that *Mohawk*'s performance was an illusion. Such small and petty arguments were demolished by Mr F. E. Smith—later Lord Birkenhead—who in one brief statement won the case—the Board had not objected to the Maplin Mile being used for the test prior to the trial; the *Mohawk* had exceeded the contract speed by one knot, therefore she had earned the bonus!

Thornycrofts certainly came out of the case better than the Admiralty.

Repeat orders were placed in the 1906–7 programme when two ships were contracted: *Amazon* by Thornycroft and *Saracen* by Whites, displacing 966 and 970 tons respectively. *Amazon* had Thornycroft boilers and *Saracen* was equipped with White-Forsters like their respective predecessors. Both had Parsons turbines and four funnels—*Saracen*'s were very stubby and later had to be raised. Not before time the puny gun armament of the earlier batch was improved upon; in these and subsequent boats it was raised to two 4-inch guns, but the torpedo armament was left unchanged. Earlier the Admiralty had objected to the heavier weapons although all the lessons digested so far had pointed to the need for something heavier than the 12-pounder.

The *Saracen* achieved 34·5 knots over the Maplin Mile but the Admiralty, still smarting about *Mohawk* no doubt, further insisted that she should re-run over Skelmorlie where her builders were forced to run three full power runs and change propellers before she made 33·168. *Amazon* ran her trials at the same speed and was the first destroyer to ship the 4-inch gun, soon to become the standard destroyer mounting.

A further five vessels were included in the 1907–8 Estimates which completed the class. These latter ships all showed yet further increases in size and displacement, being the first destroyers to top 1,000 tons, and were roughly four times the size of the *Havock* of fifteen years before! The Palmer-built *Viking* was distinguished by being the only six-funnelled ship ever built for the Royal Navy; she further distinguished herself by sinking the tug *Triton* on her maiden voyage from the Tyne!

All averaged around 33·5 knots on trial, the *Crusader* being the fastest with 34·8, her six White-Forster boilers developing 15,500 ihp. She, together with the *Viking* and *Zulu*, had bridge torpedo-firing gear while, in September 1910, *Maori* and *Crusader* were given special fitments to operate a High-Speed Anti-Submarine Sweep of which great things were expected.*

While reports from sea were full of praise for the 'Tribals', the cost per ship was too expensive for them to be repeated in large numbers and the early armament mounted was noticeably inferior to foreign vessels of much smaller displacement, which fact was much criticised. It was not until late in the First World War that the five early boats finally had their futile 12-pounders replaced. *Viking* carried a 6-inch gun for a while, which was the other extreme, but this was not a success and the 4-inch quick-fire were substituted. The 'Tribals' also adopted the 14-inch torpedo-tube for close range work in the Channel and pom-poms were fitted for anti-aircraft work.

On the outbreak of war in 1914 all the 'Tribals' were found serving in the 6th Flotilla at Dover and all had a very eventful war on this station, in and out of trouble for the entire period despite their age. But it was mainly their poor endurance which saw them thus employed, in the face of attacks by modern German destroyers, rather than any special qualities of speed or power. In fact their armaments were described by Admiral Bacon as 'useless' for the work involved. Bacon gave a graphic description of what life in a destroyer of the 6th Flotilla involved:

> The routine of the Dover destroyers was to have steam on the engines, either at sea or in harbour, for seventeen days in succession; then to spend three days laid up for boiler-cleaning,

*The term 'High Speed Sweep' should not be taken too literally for, although an improvement on existing sweep systems, which were in their infancy, it still tended to carry away at any speed in excess of ten knots.

and once every four months they had twenty days in the dock-yard for coating the ship's bottom, and making defects good. During the seventeen days, when in harbour, officers and crews remained on their vessels ready to slip instantly.

Between 17th October and 8th November 1914 the 'Tribals' found plenty of excitement bombarding the seaward flank of the German army as it established itself on the Flanders coast. On one occasion the *Crusader* was able to demolish the Hotel Majestic at Ostend which was full of General Staff Officers of the Kaiser's victorious army. On another occasion the same destroyer, in company with the ancient gunboats *Bustard* and *Excellent*, of 1870 vintage, were caught in a heavy concentration of return fire from the 8-inch batteries the Germans had quickly established. *Crusader* signalled to the gunboats: 'Cease fire and follow me at 36 knots' and drew rapidly away. When it was realised that the little gun-boats were falling behind somewhat she again enquired as to why they were not following at 36 knots to which the *Bustard*, whose best speed was 5 knots flat out, replied: 'We are'!

The enemy batteries soon made themselves felt and the *Amazon* flying the flag of Rear-Admiral Hood had a hole 8 feet square blown in her hull on the waterline from a near miss on 20th October. The first success against U-boats occurred on 4th March 1915. The *Viking* (Commander E. R. G. R. Evans, CB) sighted the *U.8* on the surface in foggy weather in the Straits. The destroyer opened fire at 1,000 yards range but the submarine dived. Joined by no less than nine other destroyers. *Viking* began to search the sea-bed patiently with her sweeping gear. Once the U-boat periscope was sighted and the sweep fired but without success. A further patient search ensued and then, after an hour, the *Maori* (Commander B. W. Barrow) again spotted the U-boat's periscope and the *Ghurka* (Lieutenant-Commander R. W. Richardson) swept across its path, located the submarine and blew it to the surface stern first. The twenty-eight officers and men were taken prisoner, but the *U.8* sank under tow.

She was soon avenged, for on 7th May the *Maori* and *Crusader* were sent in to carry out reconnaissance work off Zeebrugge. The first-named vessel struck a mine and sank close by the Weukub-gen Lightship, and two trawlers came out from Zeebrugge and took her crew prisoner. A few weeks later the *Mohawk* also struck a mine and was badly damaged, but made Dover and was subsequently repaired. Later the *Viking* was also mined and almost broken in half, the two sections of her riven hull being held in place by the shafts. Her fore section was towed into Dover and a new stern section built on. Yet another casualty from mining was the *Zulu* which had her stern blown off.

During the German destroyer raid in which the *Flirt* had been sunk (see Chapter 4, page 66.) there were six 'Tribals' ready to steam at Dover. In their haste to put to sea they became split up into two divisions of three boats each and of the first group the *Nubian* (Commander M. R. Bernard) outpaced the *Cossack* and *Amazon*. On her own then she sighted a darkened destroyer at very close range and flashed a challenge. At once six German boats swept past her at fifty yards' range firing as they went and the rear German ship put a torpedo into the *Nubian* before vanishing into the night.

The explosion blew away almost all her fo'c'sle but fortunately the Germans did not return and the remnants of the *Nubian* were taken in tow. Before she could be brought into Dover harbour the tow parted in bad weather and the hulk went ashore near the South Foreland, where the remains of her bow section parted company. After being ashore through two gales the stern section was eventually refloated and towed into Harwich dockyard where it was grafted onto the bows of the *Zulu*. The join was effected between the *Zulu's* third funnel and *Nubian's* fourth. Rebuilding took six months and then, re-equipped and named appropriately enough *Zubian* (*D.99*), she took her place back in the line of action and was credited with the destruction of the German submarine *UC.50* on 4th February 1918 thus earning the cost of her rebuild.

The *Afridi* was present when the *UB.13* was caught up in the sweep of the drifter *Gleaner*. The drifter's crew disabled the submarine with a lance bomb and the *Afridi* finished her off by firing her sweep over the spot. The *Ghurka* was the last 'Tribal' loss, being mined, like so many of the others, some four miles off Dungeness Bay on 8th February 1917 with regrettable loss of life. The others saw the war through, although the *Crusader* became one of the first of many British destroyers to be badly damaged by air attack in the Dover area.

It was obvious that with the Armistice Fisher's proud 'Tribals' had had their day and together with his other great ships, *Dread-*

nought, Indomitable and *Inflexible*, they went to the breakers between 1919 and 1920. Their nickname, however, has since passed into destroyer history with their equally large and famous successors of World War Two, although recently their proud tradition has been relegated to a class of frigates, cheaply built and armed with old destroyer guns!

* * * * *

The final remarkable craft of Fisher's remarkable era was the *Swift*. In order to achieve a 36-knotter Fisher asked for designs of 320 feet length with a tonnage of 900. Such a vessel would have been structurally unsound and so began a series of designs put forward to meet Fisher's ideal. She was to be named *Flying Scud* and she was to be the fastest thing afloat. Originally the design called for a puny armament, similar to the 'Rivers' and based on the 12-pounder, but, as the designs came in and were rejected, costs soared and the tonnage increased. The final version came out at a tonnage of 2,170 with a worthwhile armament of four 4-inch guns, two 18-inch torpedo-tubes and a length of 345 feet! Truly a ship to conjure with.

Cammell Laird, as Laird Brothers had now become, had their tender accepted, but the conditions laid down by the Admiralty were very hard, with an £18,000 penalty should contract speed not be attained. Her name was changed to *Swift* in April 1906 and she was finally launched in December the following year. Perhaps because she was unique and so much was expected of her, the speeds attributed to her—38, 39 and even 40 knots being frequently quoted—were far from realistic.

In fact Cammell Laird's had enormous difficulty in getting her to reach her contract speed and she was only eventually accepted for service in February 1910. Her best run had been 35½ knots—and this after twenty-six attempts and frequent changes of propellers. Some £44,000 in penalty money was forthcoming for lack of speed and late delivery but this was subsequently lowered to £5,000 as 'an act of grace'. Even so she cost a staggering £233,764 which ruled out any further experiments on those lines.

She was considered excellent as a scout, but was a wet steamer due to lack of flare in her bows. She was obviously out of place among the flotillas and it was fortunate that by the outbreak of war a demand had arisen for a larger boat to act as flotilla leader, as the speeds of the cruisers, normally employed in that duty, had fallen well behind the new destroyers entering service. She went to the Dover Patrol and saw much employment here. Her size allowed various liberties to be taken in experimental usages.

After a short period with the Grand Fleet, during which she was fitted with the Egerton anti-submarine sweep, *Swift* joined the 6th Flotilla at Dover and underwent various changes of armament including the shipping of a 6-inch gun. This proved more acceptable in the *Swift* than in the *Viking*, but by May 1917 the big gun was taken out and two 4-inch quick-firing re-instated. Her very flimsy bridge structure was also rebuilt.

The Modified Sweep perhaps needs some explanation. Basically it was a wire loop about 200 yards long to which were affixed wooden floats to keep it buoyant just about level with the surface. Below this was located a series of small explosive charges which were kept at a regulated depth. If a submarine was sighted but subsequently dived, this cumbersome apparatus was streamed astern the destroyer, unfortunately restricting its hunting speed to around 10 knots. If the speed was increased, the gear became fouled up or was carried away. If the sweep became entangled with any submerged obstruction, a needle registered aboard the destroyer; if the obstruction was in the likely vicinity of the submarine, the charges could be fired by pressing an electric switch. Only two submarines were definitely destroyed by a sweep and it was much loathed and detested by the crews of the ships equipped with it. Nevertheless, until 1916, it was all they had, except for their ram bows and high speed, to combat the U-boats.

Swift's big moment came on the night of the 20th April 1917 during one of the German tip-and-run raids across the Straits. Following their several successful runs the Admiral, Dover was determined to put a stop to these operations and was well prepared. Six large German boats had sortied out and, while two bombarded Calais as a diversion, four others made an attack on Dover, shelling the town for twenty minutes. They then steered north-east along the eastern edge of the Goodwin Sands. Here they were sighted some fifty minutes past midnight by the *Swift* (Commander A. M. Peck) and the *Broke* (Commander E. R. G. R. Evans).

The six German ships were approaching on an opposite, but parallel, course and fire was opened at once by both sides. Both

British ships increased speed and the *Swift* put her helm over with the intention of ramming. Unable to see for a few vital seconds, due to the flash of the 6-inch gun, Peck missed astern of the German line but managed to put a torpedo into last but one vessel, the *G.85*.

The *Broke* was more successful in her ramming attempt and caught the *G.42* amidships her guns firing into the German ship at the same time. While the *Broke* was thus engaged one of the German ships torpedoed her. Meantime the *Swift* pursued the flying German squadron until hit by a shell and forced to drop back. She rescued some survivors from the German ships and then came upon the disabled *Broke* and stood by her. Commander Peck was awarded the DSO for this action.

The *Swift* survived in service until 1922 and then went the way of so many of her sisters. She remained the largest destroyer constructed for the Royal Navy until the *Laforey* joined the Fleet in 1941.

$$* \quad * \quad * \quad * \quad *$$

Once again twelve different destroyers—thirteen if the *Swift* is included—had been sent to sea in 1905–6, of which hardly any two were similar. Commodore Lewis Bayly had been testing his boats to the limit, as the casualties aforelisted have shown, and risking the Admiralty's wrath in a sincere attempt to get to the roots of destroyer organisation and building; he submitted many original suggestions to his superiors before they moved him on to the Battle-Cruiser Force. Some ideas found little favour, such as his recommendations that destroyers should not attack an enemy fleet venturing to sea because that was what any British Admiral would want it to do, but the most cogent was a plea for uniformity among boats serving in the same squadrons, flotillas, or divisions.

The problems involved with a division of boats carrying out complicated manoeuvres when each ship had a different turning circle was immense, not to mention questions of speed, endurance and seaworthiness. Another recommendation was that every squadron should be led by a scout and here can be see the germ of the flotilla-leader idea which was not to come into practice for many years.

In view of the uncertainty of wartime supplies of oil fuel it had been decided to revert to coal fuel for the destroyers of the 1908–9 Programme, a decision based on firm foundation but one which was very highly criticised when made public, despite the fact that the Germans were still laying down boats which could exceed our best speeds and yet were still coal-fired.

Chapter VII

Standard Dimensions

The 'Beagle' Class represented the first attempt by the Admiralty to produce a homogeneous flotilla of ships, by laying down a standard specification. There were sixteen in all which allowed for four divisions of four boats each. They were ostensibly designed to counter the new German boats, but when they came out it would appear that they had fallen short on every count. Their main armament of a single 4-inch gun and three 12-pounders was lighter than the two 3·5-inch guns carried by the 560-ton German boats, while their speed, at 27 knots, was three knots slower. The torpedo armament was an improvement in that the 'Beagles' shipped the new 21-inch torpedo, soon to be the standard torpedo of the Royal Navy, but as in previous classes only two were mounted, one right aft trained over the stern, and the other forward of the after mast. This arrangement proved unsatisfactory and was not repeated. Some boats mounted a 3-pounder anti-aircraft gun which showed unexpected foresight somewhere. But altogether, on a displacement of around 960 tons, their armament was not impressive.

Shipbuilding was slack when the 'Beagles' were laid down and many of the tenders were low in order to keep the men employed. The Admiralty was harshly taken to task at the time for ruthlessly taking advantage of this fact, and indeed the useless mounting of the obsolete 12-pounder was held up as yet a further attempt to economise at the expense of efficiency. The DNC, Sir Philip Watts, received much of the blame for the apparent inferiority of the 'Beagle' design, but as has been pointed out, he was not responsible for the Board's specification. While it was expected that destroyers should show at least a seven knot excess in speed over cruisers, the 'Beagles' rated very low. They seem, however, to have been popular commands and presented a very handsome profile with three uniform funnels of equal height, although later the fore-funnel in some ships was altered.

The big improvement was the placing of the 4-inch gun on a

raised deckhouse forward which provided a superb command view. It is a thousand pities this idea was not retained for all subsequent destroyers, but it was not, and, like the retention of the wing turrets in the contemporary battleships, this was a recurring feature which marred many ships of the period. A high and dry mounting for the destroyers' armament was not to be re-introduced until the advent of the 'V' Class in 1917.

The *Basilisk* and *Harpy* were fitted with White-Forster boilers, but all the other 'Beagles' had Yarrow boilers. The *Grampus*, originally named *Nautilus*, had the distinction of being the only destroyer to be built by the Thames Ironworks at Blackwall, before high labour costs closed that firm, and she turned out to be the fastest of her class with 28·1 knots; she also had the highest bunkerage. However, *Grampus* took two years to build as compared with eighteen months for the others. All were fitted with the Parsons turbines, but the combination of the turbine and coal-firing did not work out well. The total complement in this class had risen to 104 and they carried two whalers, two gigs, a dinghy, twenty-four lifebuoys and a lifebelt for every man. The equipment was beginning to build up in destroyers and the 'Beagles' carried— as standard fitting—torpedo fore-bridge firing gear. They were also the first class to adopt the new stockless anchor.

Apart from the above mentioned failings, the 'Beagles' turned out to be good sea boats and far superior to the 'Tribals' in the matter of endurance. When completed they formed the 1st Flotilla and served at home under the command of Commodore Sir Robert Arbuthnot in the light cruiser *Boadicea*. In his autobiography Admiral Cunningham, then Lieutenant in Command of the *Scorpion*, describes the routine for the flotillas at that time:

In a cycle of four weeks the destroyers would go to sea each Monday at noon and stay out till Thursday night for three weeks in succession. On Fridays and during the fourth week we did harbour drills. In the intervals we coaled and tried to keep our ships clean. Weather made no difference. Whether it was thick fog or a gale of wind we still went to sea, even though we could do nothing in the way of gunnery or torpedo exercises, night attacks, steaming without lights, tactics, taking each other in tow, or any of the other exercises or evolutions that Sir Robert thought would be good for us. It was no wonder that the flotilla became known as the 'Outer Gabbard Yacht Club', so-called from the Outer Gabbard Lightship, well out in the North Sea, which was our usual rendezvous by day and by night. It was a hard life but we learnt a lot.

Indeed the severe training made them as fully acquainted with the dour North Sea as with the backs of their hands, which made it all the more of a loss that—when war was declared—the 'Beagles', with their experienced complements, found themselves in the Mediterranean! Here, save for a brief period, they were to remain until 1917.

Flotilla organisation was now beginning to take shape as the 'Beagles' and following classes joined the Fleet in 1910–13. It was clear who our next enemy would be, and indeed it was common knowledge on both sides of the North Sea that the Germans were husbanding coal stocks and increasing their building tempo in readiness for *'Der Tag'*—which was more imminent than most people realised.

Until 1905 all the early destroyers had been based on the three Home Ports with the few exceptions of those stationed in the Mediterranean or on the China station. At that time a Home, Channel and Atlantic Flotilla was formed with the surplus boats organised into training squadrons or tenders. This arrangement survived until 1909.*

With the abolition of the Channel Fleet in 1909, just as the first 'Beagles' were being laid down, the Home Fleet destroyers were divided into three flotillas: the 1st and 2nd consisted of the new 'Tribals' and 'Rivers' while the 3rd Flotilla comprised all the older destroyers still in commission with nucleus crews. On their completion the 'Beagles' joined the 1st Flotilla.

In the meantime Sir Lewis Bayly's recommendations on organisation had been formulated. Despite his feeling that the term 'flotilla' no longer had any meaning, it was retained but was completely reorganised as a fighting unit. The standard size of the flotilla was twenty boats which gave five divisions of four boats each. In theory this allowed for a permanent readiness with four divisions always ready for sea while the fifth was refitting and so on. Each division was further sub-divided into two-boat sub-divisions, command being according to seniority. Brooding over

* A typical composition, as listed in 1906, appears in Appendix I, page 168.

the whole flotilla would be the Captain (D) usually embarked in a Scout or Light Cruiser, although by 1914 it was realised that a more specialised ship was needed for this task and most Grand Fleet flotillas eventually had two Flotilla Leaders per twenty boats. Where more than one flotilla was in operation—the Grand Fleet at one time had six full flotillas—they were under the guidance of the Commodore (T) in a light cruiser.

Although the destroyers themselves had by this time grown into sturdy, heavily armed, ocean-going ships and very well equipped for an *offensive* role, the Admiralty still regarded their original function as the most valid. The retention of the official term 'Torpedo Boat Destroyer' showed this, although in service and in general the abbreviation to 'Destroyer' had long been commonplace. This showed also in the comparison that can be made with the German equivalents of this period, still classified as 'Torpedo Boats' although, again, their size was the equivalent of the British TBDs. The German destroyers, for so they may be termed, showed a far greater emphasis on the torpedo element. This was the reflection of the greater superiority in numbers that Great Britain still had, and was to retain, in battleships. Because of this, the disablement of some of them before the main line of battle met in combat was obviously essential to the Germans.

Conversely, because it was felt that such a battle as was then envisaged would almost certainly find the Royal Navy with a preponderance of battleship strength, and that the issue would be decided by this fact, the Admiralty naturally attached much greater importance to the role of destroyer in warding off enemy torpedo craft and leaving the field free for the battle line to make undisturbed practice. This was certainly sound, but an ever-growing emphasis was growing up in the flotillas themselves that they could carry out this duty and then, once accomplished, the logical, and to the young destroyer skippers, most desirable thing would be to attack the enemy line itself.

The ideal position striven for by the main battle fleets was the crossing of the enemy line of advance—'crossing the T'—and thus allowing for maximum broadsides into the head of the enemy column from which return fire would be limited to the forward arcs of the leading vessels. In a massed destroyer assault the position striven for was the placing of two flotillas ahead and on either side of the enemy van, thus no matter which way avoiding action was taken against one set of torpedoes, the flotilla on the opposing side would be presented with sitting targets.

Although the British boats, as we have seen, carried only a very limited torpedo armament and re-loads, this ideal attack position, if ever achieved, would have presented, with two full flotillas of sixteen boats or twenty boats engaged, an enemy battle line with converging broadsides of up to forty torpedoes on each bow, a certain percentage of which, it was felt, must cause enormous havoc to the most important ships.

Unfortunately this ideal attacking position was never achieved in wartime, for the margin of speed that the destroyers had to have to outpace the enemy battle fleet was never achieved, and bad weather further restricted it. More, the clouds of dense smoke thrown out by the myriads of attacking craft tended to obscure the range-finders of the battleships of their own side, which could not be tolerated by a predominantly gunnery-minded fleet; the resulting confusion of the clash between the battle lines of opposing destroyers further ruled out the chances of a textbook attack on these lines.

Only in manoeuvres did this setpiece flotilla attack ever work out, and then usually in night attacks. Under cover of darkness it was sometimes possible for the flotillas to work up ahead of the 'enemy' van and deal a devastating blow—a fact which may explain the cautious approach to night fighting that so decided the outcome of the Battle of Jutland.

With so many boats of the 'Beagle' and later classes presenting similar profiles, quite different to the old assortment of funnel combinations, attempts were made around 1912–13 to introduce a standard funnel band recognition code. The 'Beagles' had white (and later also red) funnel bands added at this time, but the supply of destroyers soon overtook the possible combinations and the first Pendant Numbers were adopted in 1914. On the 27th February an Admiralty Fleet Order was issued to the effect that the *Stag* (*P.06*) and the *Mallard* (*P.08*) were to paint up their temporary pendants.* (The full list of subsequent pendants and wartime alterations is given in Appendix Two.)

* Every warship carried a distinguishing number indicated by a small pendant flown at the mast. With smaller ships of the destroyer size, these pendants became hard to identify because of the smoke and spray, and the ships' low silhouette. These numbers were then painted in large white letters on the

The 'Beagles' were the last destroyers to be built to drawings prepared by specialist firms, with a few notable exceptions, and no variation was normally tolerated.

The *Nautilus* was renamed the *Grampus* in 1913 when it was decided to give the former name to a submarine.

*   *   *   *   *

The 'Beagles' were very hard worked during their war service; the name ship herself, employed on escort duty covering the movement of the BEF to France in 1914, had her boilers lit for twenty-six days out of twenty-eight. Eight 'Beagles' were at sea with Admiral Troubridge's squadron of armoured cruisers during the escape of the *Goeben* and *Breslau*, but all save three had to fall out to re-coal during the high-speed steaming to intercept them, owing to the non-arrival of their collier. The *Beagle* and *Bulldog* sailed with the *Dublin* from Malta on 6th August and accompanied her when she tried to intercept on her own after the battle cruisers had lost touch and the armoured cruisers withdrew from the hunt.

A number of 'Beagles' were present co-operating with the French fleet when it swept into the Adriatic and, with its twelve battleships, destroyed the tiny Austrian cruiser *Zenta*. 'Not', Admiral Cunningham recalled, 'a very glorious victory'. But it was in the Dardanelles that they came into their own and earned their nickname of the 'Mediterranean Beagles'. They even ran their own newspaper The *Tenedos Times* from their depot ship *Blenheim*.

Following the main bombardment of the Dardanelles on 18th March 1915, the *Basilisk*, *Grasshopper*, *Mosquito* and *Racoon* were employed in covering the minesweepers clearing the Kephez field and the two latter vessels assisted in rescuing *Irresistible*'s crew after she had been mined. During the rescue operations *Racoon* was damaged by another mine or a near-miss shell.

During the landings at Anzac Cove by the Australians on Gallipoli in April the *Beagle* (Commander H. R. Godfrey), *Bulldog* (Lieutenant-Commander W. B. Mackenzie), *Foxhound* (Commander W. G. Howard) and *Scourge* (Lieutenant-Commander H. de B. Tupper) were employed with considerable success. At the same

---

forward section of the hull and also on the stern for rapid identification. However, in order to confuse the enemy, the pendant numbers were frequently changed throughout the war.

time several were fitted out as 'high-speed' minesweepers after the failure of the drifters to clear a path; they were sent back into the Straits to sweep a channel so that big ships could close the coast and provide fire support. This task was described subsequently as:

> Not very pleasant paddling along at 12 knots against a 2 or 3 knot current, tied by the tail to another destroyer and being fairly constantly straddled by the salvoes from those high-velocity guns.

Damage was inevitable; *Racoon* took a shell in her boiler room, *Mosquito* was hit, causing heavy casualties and the *Wolverine* was struck full on the bridge and her Captain, Commander O. J. Prentis, was killed. They were fully employed during the following period in this theatre providing short range fire support which they did with great success, the *Scorpion* on one occasion surprising two Turkish battalions in the light of her searchlights and slaughtering some three hundred of them in concentrated fire. At Suvla Bay, too, the 'Beagles' were fully extended and the six mentioned, together with the *Arno*, towed ashore a landing barge each with 500 men aboard while another 500 were aboard the destroyers themselves. These were landed on 6th–7th August 1915, but a similar assault force of troops aboard the *Beagle*, *Bulldog* and *Grampus* went ashore at the wrong point. The sole casualty was the *Scourge*, hit in the boiler room by a heavy shell.

During the subsequent evacuations at both Anzac and Suvla on the nights of 18th, 19th and 20th December, the *Wolverine*, *Grasshopper*, *Bulldog* and others took part. This was followed by the blockade of the Aegean in which the 'Beagles' had a part. Although half the flotilla had returned to home waters in 1915, these all subsequently rejoined the Mediterranean Fleet, finally returning to home waters in 1917.

Of the sixteen boats only three were lost and all these by accident rather than enemy action. The *Wolverine* was lost in a collision off north-west Ireland on 12th December 1917 and a mere three weeks later her sister the *Racoon* went aground in a blinding snowstorm and was lost with all hands. The *Pincher* was wrecked on the Seven Stones on 24th July 1918. The remainder of the class—the last coal-burning destroyers actually *built* for the Royal Navy—were broken up in the years 1921 and 1922.

*   *   *   *   *

There was a general reaction against the coal-burning 'Beagles' when the destroyer-building programme for 1909–10 was discussed and the twenty boats of the resulting 'Acorn' Class were better value for money in every way than their predecessors. Tonnage was only 760; armament increased to two 4-inch guns and two 12-pounders with two 21-inch torpedo-tubes. The reason a heavier armament could be carried by a smaller ship was of course the final abandonment of coal in favour of oil fuel, 170 tons being carried.

All the 'Acorns' were built with Parsons turbines except the *Brisk* which had Brown Curtis turbines fitted at a cost of an extra £3,000 per set. All had Yarrow boilers except for the *Redpole, Rifleman* and *Ruby*, built by Whites, which had White-Forster boilers. A sea speed of 27 knots was again accepted, and this they all achieved comfortably enough, the fastest boat being the *Ruby* with 29·371 knots.

The original designs provided for reciprocating engines at one time but this retrograde step was soon cancelled. The costs worked out at between £86,835 for Thornycroft's *Minstrel* up to £103,882 for the Clydebank's *Brisk*. A few mounted a 3-pounder AA gun. They turned out to be excellent sea boats despite some early forbodings over their high tonnage, the increased flare of their bows being responsible for this. They had a high roomy chart-house topped by an open bridge. Faithful to Fisher's principles, the forefunnel was completed below bridge level which very soon had to be altered; Oscar Parkes recorded that, with the one tall thin round funnel and the two broad oval ones, they were known in the service as 'the Woodbine and two Gyppie boats'.

As the design had been prepared by the Admiralty a wider range of builders was able to compete for destroyer building, which spread experience into yards which subsequently became famous for their destroyers, but which left others of high skill, like Yarrows, out in the cold, although their yards were always full of boats building for foreign navies.

An improved mark of the 21-inch torpedo was carried which had a speed to range ratio of 30 knots to 10,800 yards, which was thought to be far ahead of any rival weapon. Heavy weather damage in June 1911 necessitated some strengthening of the hull, but otherwise there were few obvious shortcomings to the 'Acorns'. They were formed into the 2nd Flotilla and were duly given red funnel bands during the 1911–13 experiments in identification.

*　　*　　*　　*　　*

The 'Acorns' served with the Grand Fleet until around 1915 when many went to the Mediterranean. In September 1917 the *Minstrel* and *Nemesis* were loaned to the Japanese Navy for escort duties in that theatre, being returned in 1919. A pre-war proposal to replace the forward 4-inch gun with a 4·7-inch was not followed up, but the *Nymph* was fitted with depth-charge racks and throwers later in the war.

Staunch took part in the evacuation of Gallipoli in December 1915 and continued to serve in the Mediterranean until sunk by a U-boat off Gaza on 11th November 1917. The *Goldfinch* went aground in fog on Sanday Island in the Orkneys on the night of the 18th–19th February 1915. The *Comet* was also lost in the Mediterranean being sunk by a U-boat on 6th August 1918. The remainder of the 'Acorns' were sold to Wards in June 1921, except for *Minstrel* which lingered until early the following year and *Hope* and *Martin,* sold in Malta in 1920.

*　　*　　*　　*　　*

Experience with the 'Acorns' and the 'Beagles' showed the advantages of oil fuel over coal and the suggestion that destroyers should be coal-fired was only raised once more. This occurred in November 1915 when there was a fear of grave shortage of oil fuel. An improved 'Beagle' design was mooted, to be armed with three 4-inch guns and two torpedo-tubes, but the idea was dropped because it would have required an increase in the complement per ship. 'Taffrail' summed up the blessings of oil fuel:

> Oil had many advantages. It lessened the strain on the personnel when steaming at high speeds, when every ounce of coal had to be shovelled into the furnaces; reduced the numbers of men necessary in the boiler-rooms; and made the task of refuelling much easier. In the older method of 'coaling ship' every pound of coal had to be dug out of the hold of a collier, shovelled into bags, and then hoisted on board the ship and tipped down into her bunkers. It was a laborious, exhausting business, which took much time. In a ship burning oil fuel, however, she merely goes alongside an oiler, connects up a few hoses, and the pumps do the rest.

Chapter VIII

Reversion to Speed

Some of the lessons to be learned from the operations of the 'Beagles' and 'Acorns' were indeed assimilated. In the next batch of destroyers to be laid down under the gradually accelerating building programme of the years leading up to August 1914, the specification called for oil-burners with bunkerage for an extra 30 tons of fuel oil. This was the 'Acheron' Class—as the 'Improved Acorns' were soon to be known. The other notable advance was to improve weather resistance by extending the fo'c'sle and setting the bridge itself some nine feet further aft. In other respects their dimensions were exactly as the 'Acorns' with displacements of around 760 tons. Of the twenty vessels laid down under the 1910–11 Programme, fourteen of them were to the rigid Admiralty specification, but, in order to try and gain some improvement over the 'Acorn' performance figures, the remaining six were tendered out to specialist firms as in the old days. They were allowed some leeway over the standard boats in the hope that they might be able to present a vessel similar in all respects to the rest of the class but with an extra knot or so to counter the 30-knot standard now attained throughout the German destroyer programmes. These six were *Archer* and *Attack*, from Yarrow; *Acheron* and *Ariel*, from Thornycroft; and *Badger* and *Beaver* which were awarded to Parsons, the hulls being constructed by Denny Brothers of Dumbarton. The 'specials' came out with slightly enlarged displacements, the Yarrow and Thornycroft boats being around the 770-ton mark and the Parsons boats over 800 tons.

The majority of the twenty boats had Parsons turbines but the Yarrow boats and the three John Brown-built boats—*Hind*, *Hornet* and *Hydra*—shipped Brown-Curtis with two shafts. In 1910 Parsons developed the semi-geared turbine. As before the low-pressure turbine acted directly, but an extension of gear wheels was fitted driven by a smaller, high-pressure turbine. This arrangement was intended, by single reduction, to provide for a more economical distribution of power with the bonus of an increased radius of action. By 1912 fully geared turbines had been fitted to two of the 'L' Class boats giving a single reduction gearing from high and low power turbines acting on each gearing. An estimated improvement in efficiency of some twenty per cent was thus achieved, but, due to a shortage of suitable gear-cutting equipment capable of producing work to the fine tolerances required, there was considerable delay in its general introduction. After 1915 this single reduction gearing became standard fitting for all destroyers. The *Badger* and *Beaver* adopted the new, semi-geared Parsons. On trials, average speeds for the 'ordinaries' came out between a poor 26·9 for the *Jackal* to 30·1 for the *Ferret*.

The armament was the same as the 'Acorns' with just the two single tubes and two further torpedoes carried. Both the *Beaver* and the *Tigress* were involved in accidents during their trial period which delayed their acceptance into service. All save the *Hydra* were launched in 1911 and on joining the fleet they formed the 1st Flotilla and were allocated red and white funnel bands. The fore-funnel was raised in many of these ships, around 1917, due to the usual problems of smoke. As completed both were of equal height, below bridge level, although the Yarrow-built boats had theirs spaced farther from the bridge in an effort to alleviate this failing.

They were reported to be economical steamers and also had excellent handling qualities. On trials the six specials proved slightly superior with speeds ranging from 29·4 for the *Acheron* up to the *Badger*'s 30·7 knots. The fitting of an improved super-heater—superheating was a Yarrow device to increase the fuel economy of the boilers—was responsible for the ten to fifteen per cent improvement in economy, depending on speed.

* * * * *

At the outbreak of war the 'Acheron' Class formed the 1st Flotilla at Harwich and was involved in much action in the ensuing three years before they left that command. In order to illustrate the composition of a typical flotilla at the outbreak of war the line of battle of the First Flotilla was made up as follows:

Light Cruiser: *Fearless* (Captain W. F. Blunt)
1st Division: *Acheson* (Commander B. M. Money)
           Attack (Lieutenant-Commander C. Callaghan)
           Hind (Lieutenant-Commander G. Corlett)
           Archer (Lieutenant-Commander H. F. Littledale)

2nd Division: *Ariel* (Commander D. E. Moir)
     Hydra (Lieutenant-Commander R. J. Buchanan)
     Hornet (Commander C. G. Chichester)
     Tigress (Lieutenant-Commander P. Whitfield)

3rd Division: *Ferret* (Commander G. Mackworth)
     Forester (Lieutenant-Commander M. G. B. Legge)
     Druid (Lieutenant-Commander E. J. G. MacKinnon)
     Defender (Lieutenant-Commander W. J. Fletcher)

4th Division: *Badger* (Commander C. A. Freemantle)
     Beaver (Lieutenant-Commander K. A. Beattie)
     Jackal (Lieutenant-Commander J. C. Hodgson)
     Sandfly (Lieutenant-Commander F. G. C. Coates)

5th Division: *Goshawk* (Commander the Hon. H. Meade)
     Lizard (Lieutenant-Commander E. C. O. Thomson)
     Lapwing (Lieutenant-Commander A. H. Gye)
     Phoenix (Lieutenant-Commander M. K. H. Kennedy)

Also in the Harwich Force, under the command of Commodore (T) Reginald Tyrwhitt, who was flying his flag in the light cruiser *Amethyst*, was the 3rd Flotilla, twenty destroyers of the brand-new 'L' Class, led by the *Amphion* and the Depot Ship *Maidstone*. Commodore (S) Roger Keyes, CB, MVO—whom we last met in the *Fame*—was responsible for some eight submarines which he led with typical dash from either the *Firedrake* or the *Lurcher*, two destroyers specially attached.

The 1st Flotilla soon saw action. On 16th August, after a night spent close inshore off the mouth of the Ems deep in the Heligoland Bight, some of its divisions were surprised at first light by the Armoured Cruiser *Yorck*. She immediately laid down a heavy fire with her 8·2-inch guns and *Hind* was straddled while both *Goshawk* and *Phoenix* were hit. Eventually they evaded the big cruiser and came clear. Such was the rigidity of the orders of the time that not one of the destroyers went in to make a torpedo attack on the lone cruiser, who could never have dealt with the whole flotilla. This was because an order was in force at that time that destroyers were forbidden to attack heavily armed ships in daylight! For decades the torpedo had been the weapon for use in mass night attacks and despite the increased range of the weapon, and the eagerness of the destroyer men to use them at such a prime target, it had been felt necessary to issue such instructions. Thus was a fine opportunity thrown away.

The *Hind* got involved in some very complicated dealings in Ostend, just before the port was occupied by the Germans, and her two companions *Lizard* and *Lapwing* carried out a shoot at enemy positions along the Belgian coast on 21st August.

On the 28th, both flotillas took part in the sweep which resulted in the Battle of the Bight. The plan to destroy the local German patrols off Heligoland in the hope of luring out something larger worked perfectly well but in this first major action of the war many mistakes were made, not the least of which was the sending in so close to the hostile coast of the brand-new light cruiser *Arethusa* which had only been in commission one day!

During the confused scramble which started at 0700 with the sighting of a single German destroyer and ended some six hours later with the withdrawal of the British force, the 1st Flotilla was in the thick of the fighting. Between them the 3rd and 5th Divisions trapped the German destroyer *V.187* and pounded her into a smoking wreck. Not wishing to continue the very one-sided slaughter they ceased fire and sent their boats away to pick up survivors, but the German boat immediately put a shell into the *Goshawk*'s wardroom whereupon she was finished off.

The *Arethusa* was very roughly handled by the German cruisers which now came upon the scene and only one gun was left in action. Some of the German cruisers turned their attentions to the destroyers engaged upon their rescue work and the *Defender* was forced to abandon her boat, which, fortunately, was sighted by the submarine *E.4*.

The arrival of a British light cruiser squadron now caused some confusion as it was taken to be the enemy. Tyrwhitt had not been told of their addition to the scheme, but by 1000 the damaged *Arethusa* was limping home accompanied by *Fearless* and both flotillas. At this juncture, two German light cruisers appeared from the south-east and took the British ship under fire. The destroyers drove them off one at a time but they were taken for the armoured cruisers and Beatty, waiting with his battle cruisers to the north, was asked for support.

The *Strassburg* was attacked by two divisions of the 3rd flotilla and forced to turn away; the *Acheron, Attack, Hind* and *Archer* of the 1st Division arrived in time to carry out a further attack, which afforded *Arethusa* a short respite. Meantime the rest of the 1st Flotilla, led by the *Ariel*, had run into the light cruiser *Mainz* and she instantly engaged the destroyers with heavy and accurate fire. *Ferret, Defender* and *Phoenix* all got in torpedo attacks but the *Mainz* was not disturbed and continued to drive the destroyers north. Fortunately the arrival of the 1st Light Cruiser Squadron made her turn away before any of the destroyers had been hit, but in doing so she ran into the crippled *Arethusa* again and, when attacked by a defending division of the 3rd Flotilla, she punished them severely. But that was the end of *Mainz*'s good luck.

Hit by one of the destroyers' torpedoes and surrounded by six light cruisers and thirty destroyers the *Mainz* was soon a wreck and the *Firedrake* and *Lurcher* ran alongside to embark survivors. This danger over, the *Köln* and *Strassburg* reappeared and were immediately engaged by the *Fearless* leading the *Goshawk, Lizard* and *Phoenix*. Fortunately the arrival of Beatty with his great ships carried the day and his squadron's 13·5-inch salvoes soon destroyed two of the German cruisers and drove away the others. Thus the Bight turned out a British victory, for the Germans had lost three cruisers and a destroyer without return, and this in their own backyard. However, bad staff work had caused confusion on the British side and the length of time taken to demolish one outnumbered German cruiser, the *Mainz*, did not reflect much honour on our gunnery.

In October on the chance of catching German submarines leaving for their patrol areas the 2nd Division of 1st Flotilla was sent to patrol off the Terschelling Lightship. The sea was rough, darkness had closed in and visibility was poor, but a U-boat was sighted by the leading vessel, the *Badger*, and Commander Freemantle had no hesitation in ramming. Although the destroyer appeared to have struck the submarine fair and square, a search by the *Beaver, Hydra* and *Hind* revealed no trace of survivors. However, it was later found that the U-boat had suffered only light superficial damage and she returned to port safely. By contrast the *Badger* fractured her stem in the 13-knot impact, and her bows concertina'd up to the forward bulkhead. As a result of this failure the stems of all destroyers then building were considerably strengthened. Apart from the modified sweep, ramming was for a long period the only form of attack against submarines open to our destroyers. The original anti-submarine device for destroyers had been a single sweep towed with davits from the stern of the destroyer over the suspected area. Once it became entangled in a possible target the gun-cotton charges were electrically fired. Various modifications were tried to this system including the fitting of paravanes. Later the 'Combined' or 'D Sweep' was used against submarines and mines alike, but the introduction of the depth-charge rapidly rendered this slow, primitive method obsolete.

The next major engagement was the Battle of the Dogger Bank on the 24th January 1915 when fourteen destroyers of the 1st Flotilla were present, led by the *Aurora*. The pell-mell flight of the German force prevented the flotillas from making an attack. When the *Lion* was hit, the *Attack* was called alongside to enable Admiral Beatty to continue the chase. 'The good seamanship of Lieutenant Commander Cyril Callaghan in placing his vessel alongside the *Lion* and subsequently the *Princess Royal*, enabled the transfer of flag to be made in the shortest possible time', read the despatch of Admiral Beatty afterwards.

Early in February 1915 the 1st Flotilla, together with the Depot Ship *Woolwich*, transferred from Harwich to South Queensferry where they were attached to the Battle Cruiser Squadron based there. Up in these northern waters in the winter months the 'Acherons' saw further action and much bad-weather duty. On one occasion, as described by Commander Bingham of the *Hornet*, his sub-divisional mate the *Tigress* (Lieutenant Commander P. Whitfield) caught a huge wave on the 'wrong stride':

> The *Tigress* encountered one of these enormous seas, which struck her fair and with sufficient force to drive the bridge rails about four feet aft on the compass and to pin her captain between the two. He broke a rib and sustained some internal damage, yet nevertheless continued in command.

A long U-boat hunt took place on 6th–10th March. The U-boat was first sighted by a patrolling trawler north-west of Aberdeen, but due to a wireless failure the ship was unable to report until the next day. At once the destroyers were despatched to search for her and during the next few days she was spotted in various locations apparently heading determinedly for the Firth of Forth, perhaps in the hopes of getting one of Beatty's ships.

On the morning of the 10th, after the hunt had been in progress for four days, the *U.12* was sighted on the surface off Fife Ness by three of the Rosyth-based destroyers of the 1st Flotilla, *Acheron, Attack* and *Ariel*. Approaching at high speed the destroyers opened fire and hit the submarine in the conning tower; nevertheless, she dived as the *Attack* passed over her. Within a short time the *Ariel* (Lieutenant-Commander J. V. Creagh) spotted her periscope about 200 yards to starboard and turned to ram. She struck the U-boat just as it was in the process of surfacing, the earlier damage needing attention. As in the case of the *Badger*, the *Ariel* received considerable damage from this attack, the whole of her bottom plating was ripped open almost to amidships. The submarine sank right away although ten survivors were picked up. *Ariel* reached harbour, but repairs took three weeks to complete.

Barry Bingham and the *Hornet* were in the news again in October. The cruiser *Argyll*, en route to Scapa Flow from Devonport, ran aground in thick weather on Bell Rock off Dundee during a south-east gale. The *Hornet* and *Jackal* were on patrol in the Firth as usual and received instuction to stand by the stricken vessel.

They reached the *Argyll* at dawn and found her firmly wedged on the rocks and in danger of breaking up. A gale was still blowing and the big cruisers' bows were lifting and rocking with the sea which was still running wildly. The cruiser's captain suggested an immediate ferrying of his crew from the cruiser to the destroyers but Bingham felt that time was not sufficient.

Rolling and pitching in the spume and spray, the tiny destroyer was inched up until her fo'c'sle came alongside the *Argyll*'s quarter-deck. Fenders were lowered as the two vessels threatened to grind into each other. By a splendid piece of seamanship, Bingham held *Hornet* in position by her engines while the cruiser's crew jumped in batches whenever the gap closed sufficiently. With the rocks almost under her own bows and the *Argyll*'s high hull menacing her frail plates, the *Hornet* managed to embark no less than 500 men in this manner before, crammed to capacity, Bingham was forced to back his ship out. The *Jackal* then took the remainder off in boats and not a single man was lost. The only damage *Hornet* sustained was some holed and buckled plates on her starboard bow.

At the Battle of Jutland nine of the 'Acherons' were present in the 1st Flotilla, many having been replaced by the new 'M' Class boats. They were screening the 5th Battle Squadron during their famous duel with the German battle cruisers. The ships present were the *Acheron* (Commander C. Ramsey), *Ariel* (Lieutenant-Commander A. Tippet), *Attack* (Lieutenant-Commander C. James), *Hydra* (Lieutenant-Commander F. Glossop), *Badger* (Commander C. Freemantle), *Goshawk* (Commander D. Moir) and *Defender*) Lieutenant-Commander L. Palmer). With two 'L' boats they were led as always by the *Fearless* (Captain (D) C. Roper).

During the engagement, as the Grand Fleet was seen in its deployment, the shells from Hipper's great ships of the German High Seas Fleet fell around the 1st Flotilla and the *Attack* took an 11-inch shell in her wardroom. The *Defender* was also hit at this time by a heavy calibre shell which fortunately failed to explode after ricocheting into her foremost boiler room. The shell lodged itself in the ashpit of the furnace, killing a stoker petty officer and putting that boiler out of action, but it was a fortunate let-off for the tiny vessel.

Lieutenant-Commander Palmer turned out of line between the two engaged fleets and, putting the fires out, placed a collision mat over the shell hole. Once repairs had been completed they stood by the crippled destroyer *Onslow*. Tow was made with a wire hawser during which time a few stray projectiles landed close by but, at 12 knots, they got under way to the west.

During the night the sea got up and at about 1 am the next day—1st June—the tow parted. Although *Onslow* managed a few miles under her own power, by 1700 *Defender* again had to take her under tow—and again in the mounting sea the two parted. Chaincable was then passed into the *Onslow* and at eight knots the long tow was resumed. Finally at 0100 on 2nd June they made landfall opposite Aberdeen. For his endurance and determination in bringing home a crippled companion Lieutenant-Commander Palmer was awarded the DSO.

The Battle Cruiser *Invincible* flying the flag of Rear-Admiral Hood was the third casualty our heavy ships suffered during the battle. At 6.34 pm a heavy shell penetrated the roof of 'Q' Turret and she blew up instantly, breaking in half and sinking in two portions. Only six of her crew of over a thousand survived, being picked up soon after 7 pm by the *Badger*. The 1st Flotilla was not otherwise engaged.

The flotilla remained with the Grand Fleet until late in 1916 when they went to Portsmouth, although several of the 'Acherons' went out to the Mediterranean early in 1917. Here the *Attack*, on

30th December 1917 off Alexandria, and the *Phoenix*, on 14th May 1918, were both torpedoed and sunk.

In February 1918 the 20th (Minelaying) Flotilla was formed at Immingham from a variety of destroyers of various classes, including three 'Acherons', the *Ariel* (Lieutenant Rothera), *Sandfly* (Lieutenant-Commander E. H. Dauglish) and the *Ferret* (Lieutenant A. H. L. Terry). The flotilla's main duties were to lay mines inside the enemy's swept channels, a job which can be described as anything but boring! The destroyers were fitted out with minerails on sponsons aft, with winches, and were equipped to carry forty 'H2' mines and sinkers. They also laid 'M sinkers', the first magnetic mines, off Zeebrugge.

Not surprisingly in extremely hazardous work of this nature, losses, when they occurred, were heavy. The *Sandfly* was on one occasion rammed by the *Telemachus* in thick fog and her boiler room flooded. A tow lasting thirty-six hours in enemy waters finally got both ships home. The biggest disaster the flotilla suffered was on the night of 2nd–3rd August when they ran into an unsuspected German minefield. The *Vehement*, fifth ship in line, struck a mine and her forward magazine detonated blowing her bow section asunder. She was taken in tow by the *Abdiel* but while this was in progress the *Ariel* also struck a mine. Again a magazine blew up and in fifteen minutes the little ship had sunk.

The final episode of note occurred two days before the Armistice when the ancient battleship *Britannia* was torpedoed and sunk off Cape Trafalgar. The *Defender* was on hand and took off many of the crew. Not a man was lost.

Along with so many other destroyers the surviving 'Acherons' were sold to Wards Shipbreaking Company in June 1921.

*   *   *   *   *

To revert to 1911, when the 'Acorns' were building and the 'Acherons' were laid down strictly to Admiralty policy, Alfred Yarrow attempted to draw the First Lord's attention to the absurdity of this building programme which, in his view, was creating a destroyer force which could neither catch the German destroyers nor run away from them. The latest German vessels of the *G.174* type were averaging $32\frac{1}{2}$ knots against our 27–28, but the Admiralty held firm to the conviction that strength and seaworthiness would have to be sacrificed to attain such speeds. No-body had forgotten the *Cobra*.

It was not until the arrival of Admiral Jellicoe at the Con-troller's Office that Yarrow was able to obtain a sympathetic ear. He convinced that worthy that he could not only build destroyers to his own design which would be capable of reaching a guaran-teed 32 knots, but emphasised that these vessels would be fully as seaworthy as the others and fit for North Sea working. Jellicoe said that as Yarrow and Thornycroft were the specialist firms he would place an order for three such 'specials'. Yarrows turned in the best designs and the contract was duly awarded. The *Firedrake*, *Lurcher* and *Oak* were the result. With an overall length of 262 feet, a displacement of 765 tons and Parsons turbines of 20,000 horsepower, these three vessels turned out cheaper than the stan-dard boats at £91,000. Similar in layout to the 'Acherons' they had greater rake to their funnels and overall more flare to the hull and were quite distinctive.

On their trials the *Lurcher* was the fastest with 35·345 knots, a staggering performance and one that was fully maintained in service. The *Firedrake* attained 33·17 and the *Oak* 32·38 knots. After these results there was some change of mind in official circles and the war, which soon followed their completion, quickly proved their strength in all conditions. During the famous flotilla race of 1912 from Bantry Bay to the Eddystone Light, over an eighty-mile section of the passage, the 'Blue Riband' of the British Fleet was taken by *Lurcher* against all comers, her nearest competitor being left five miles astern!

*   *   *   *   *

The *Oak* was to spend the entire war as tender to the Fleet Flag-ship, *Iron Duke* and *Queen Elizabeth* in that order, and never missed a single sortie throughout that time. She was commanded by the same captain for her entire life, Commander Douglas Faviell. In a letter sent to Yarrow on 4th November 1917 he wrote:

> It may interest you to know that we still bear the reputation of never having had a breakdown which disabled the ship, never having missed a single operation with the Grand Fleet, and never having had to go to a dockyard or other repair base, except for our periodical refit. All examinations and adjust-ments have been carried out for the first seven months at an

hour's notice, and since then at two hours' notice, for full speed. The ship can still get 33 knots in spite of all the extra weight built into her since leaving your hands.

So much for strength, speed and staying power. The *Oak* had the honour of conveying the German Naval delegation to the *Queen Elizabeth* on the surrender of the High Seas Fleet to Admiral Beatty. She was finally sold in 1922.

Firedrake and *Lurcher* went to Harwich as tenders to the 8th Submarine Flotilla and, as an old destroyer hand of some repute, Commodore Keyes' method of operating his flotilla was to lead them at sea in his fast destroyers into the thick of the action, instead of directing operations from his desk ashore. Thus both destroyers saw a considerable amount of action during the war. *Firedrake* was commanded by Lieutenant-Commander A. B. Watts, and later by Commander A. Tillard; *Lurcher* initially by Commander W. Tomkinson, followed by Lionel Dawson.

*   *   *   *   *

On 27th August, just before the Battle of the Bight, Commodore Keyes had led some of his submarines into the positions allocated to them off the German coast. Next day, when the battle took place, the *Lurcher* was at one time reported lost having driven in almost to the mouth of the Ems in search of the German forces. With the *Firedrake* she searched the area for submarines and then managed to get into the fight itself. When the *Mainz* was finally silenced after her very gallant fight it was the *Lurcher* which ran alongside the smoking, burning hulk and embarked no less than 220 of the survivors. When the German cruiser finally rolled over and sank, the British destroyer narrowly escaped damage from her propellers as her stern canted up for the final plunge.

With *Firedrake* the *Lurcher* stood by and helped escort home the damaged *Laurel* and *Liberty* to end a crowded day. She was at sea with her submarines again on 23rd March 1915 during the air attacks on Borkum made by the Harwich Force.

The normal duties of the two boats were described by Captain Dawson who served aboard the *Lurcher* later on in that year:

Before *Melampus* joined us we were always alternately at instant notice for steam, or at two hours'. For any warlike operation one of us was nearly always the first ship in the port to get to sea, usually carrying Captain Waitsell on board. This had the added advantage that we were also usually the first home, since the captain had to get back to his base as soon as possible.

In the intervals of active-service operations one of us went out almost daily to provide a target upon which the submarine captains, not out on patrol, kept their eyes in. We used to carry out this practice under the protection of the numerous sandbanks with which the approach to Harwich is surrounded, and where there was a sufficient depth of water to allow a submarine to dive.

We always expected 'Fritz' to join in the proceedings and one day he very nearly did. On 27th April 1916, *UC.5* lost her way in the network of shoals and minefields and, stranding on the sandbank which was one of the boundaries of our exercising-ground, her crew were taken prisoner and brought in by the *Firedrake*.

Among other duties these two destroyers were employed in providing escorts for new submarines which had to sail to join their flotilla at Harwich from the ports of completion, mainly the Vickers yard at Barrow. Protection was needed for the submarines, not so much because of German action as for resistance to the many and various British ships eager to sink a submarine, no matter what her nationality!

Lurcher also managed to get shot at during Hipper's bombardment of Lowestoft and both ships were at sea with their submarines during the Battle of Jutland but this was in connection with an independent operation and, incredibly, no use was made of the subs to intercept the returning German Fleet.

Together with most of her contemporaries the *Lurcher* was sold for scrap in 1922 followed by the *Firedrake*. Their obvious superiority over the Admiralty boats was to lead to further demand for similar high-speed vessels in subsequent programmes.

Chapter IX

The Growing Crisis

In the years 1910–11 the Germans started to build destroyers at an accelerated rate and were soon claiming construction speeds of twelve to fifteen months for each ship. Their armament was inferior to the 'Acorn' Class, but was at least standardised for all their ships: two 3·5-inch guns and three 17·7-inch torpedoes. Generally the German destroyers, rated officially as 'Large Torpedo-Boats', were smaller than their British contemporaries, averaging around six or seven hundred tons, but in every class, from the 'S.138' of 1906 onwards, their speed was rated considerably higher. The 'V.186' Class, nearing completion in 1911, were rated as 35·3-knotters from 18,000 horsepower and, in addition, shipped *four* torpedo-tubes. Some doubts as to whether these speeds were true, or only achieved on light displacement trials, were expressed, but from experience in the war there would appear to be no doubt that the German boats were in fact two or three knots faster than ours at this time.

Although it was strongly expected that the 'S.13' Class of 690 tons were to be 36-knotters, the greatest dismay was felt when it was announced that their armament was to be two 4·1-inch and one 3·5-inch gun plus four 19·7-inch torpedo-tubes. On their small displacement and coupled with their expected high speed, they would be formidable opponents. However, it was still generally felt by the Admiralty that good gun armament, seaworthiness and low cost were the prime requirements for destroyer construction.

It was obvious that some increase in the calibre of the main armament would have to be forced upon their reluctant Lordships and for the 1911–12 Programme it was finally decided to replace the useless 12-pounders and mount a uniform armament with the subsequent advantages of ammunition supply and so on. Tests against the old *Ferret* showed that damage caused by a single 4-inch shell equalled that caused by no less than six hits from a 12-pounder. The puny torpedo armament, however, was still adhered

a. *Nubian*, two years later than *Tartar* and also from Thornycroft. Note her heightened ᴍsts and curved bows

b. *Zubian*, the composite destroyer built from the remains of *Zulu* and *Nubian*. Note her ᴀndant number and the cap on her fore-funnel

31. *Rattlesnake*, built by the London and Glasgow Shipbuilding Company in 1910—note her torpedo tube aft and her curious funnel arrangement

TABLE 9: The 'Beagle' Class

Sixteen ships, completed 1909–10. Their average displacement was 960 tons with a speed of 27 knots. Their dimensions were standardised at approximately 270 feet × 27 feet × 9 feet. Armament: one 4-inch gun; three 12-pounders; two 18-inch torpedo-tubes.

Name	Builder
Basilisk	White
Beagle	John Brown
Bulldog	John Brown
Foxhound	John Brown
Grampus	Thames Ironworks (Originally the Nautilus and renamed in 1913)
Grasshopper	Fairfield
Harpy	White
Mosquito	Fairfield
Pincher	Denny
Racoon	John Brown
Rattlesnake	Harland & Wolf
Renard	John Brown
Savage	Thornycroft
Scorpion	Fairfield
Scourge	Hawthorn Leslie
Wolverine	Cammell Laird

Ultimate disposal: *Wolverine* was sunk in collision off Lough Swilley, 1917; *Racoon* was wrecked in a storm in 1918; *Pincher* was also wrecked off the Scilly Isles in 1918; all the others were sold 1920–21.

TABLE 10: The 'Acorn' Class

Twenty ships, completed 1910–11; average displacement of 780 tons; speed 28 knots; average dimensions 240 feet × 25½ feet × 8½ feet. Armament: two 4-inch guns; two 12-pounders; two 21-inch torpedo-tubes.

Name	Builder
Acorn	John Brown
Alarm	John Brown
Brisk	John Brown
Cameleon	Fairfield
Comet	Fairfield
Fury	Inglis
Goldfinch	Fairfield
Hope	Swan Hunter
Larne	Thornycroft
Lyra	Thornycroft
Martin	Thornycroft
Minstrel	Thornycroft
Nemesis	Hawthorn Leslie
Nereide	Hawthorn Leslie
Nymphe	Hawthorn Leslie
Redpole	White
Rifleman	White
Ruby	White
Sheldrake	Denny
Staunch	Denny

Ultimate disposal: *Staunch* was sunk by a U-boat off Gaza in 1917; *Goldfinch* was wrecked in the Orkneys, 1915; *Comet* was sunk by a U-boat in the Mediterranean, 1918; all the others were sold 1920–21.

33. *Alarm*, built by Clydebank in 1910—her fore-funnel has been raised and capped against smoke; she has a searchlight on her bridge

34. *Savage*, built by Thornycroft in 1
4-inch gun mounted on a platform

s. Note her rounded funnels and the

TABLE 11: The 'Acheron' Class

Twenty-three ships, completed in 1911–13. Their average displacement was 770 tons (Specials 790 tons) with a speed of 29 knots (Specials 32–33 knots). Average dimensions were 240 feet × 25¾ feet × 9 feet. Armament: two 4-inch guns; two 12-pounders; two 21-inch torpedo-tubes.

Name	Builder	Name	Builder
Acheron	Thornycroft	*Goshawk*	Beardmore
Archer	Yarrow	*Hind*	John Brown
Ariel	Thornycroft	*Hornet*	John Brown
Attack	Yarrow	*Hydra*	John Brown
Badger	Hawthorn Leslie	*Jackal*	Hawthorn Leslie
Beaver	Hawthorn Leslie	*Lapwing*	Cammell Laird
Defender	Denny	*Lizard*	Cammell Laird
Druid	Denny	*Phoenix*	Vickers
Ferret	White	*Sandfly*	Swan Hunter
Forester	White	*Tigress*	Hawthorn Leslie

'Specials'	
Firedrake	Yarrow
Lurcher	Yarrow
Oak	Yarrow

Ultimate disposal: *Attack* was mined in the Mediterranean in 1917; *Ariel* was mined in the North Sea, 1918; *Phoenix* was sunk by a U-boat in the Adriatic, 1918; the others were sold 1920–22.

35. *Tigress*, built by Hawthorn Leslie in 1911—she has ram bows and a funnel band

36. Hawthorn Leslie's *Beaver* in 1912

7. And the *Oak*, built by Yarrow in 1913—one of the fastest destroyers in the Royal Navy

39. *Lochinvar*, built by Beardmore—a good example of a three-funnelled 'L' Class boat. Her pendant number is on her bow

TABLE 12: The 'Acasta' Class

Twenty ships, completed in 1912–13. Their average displacement was 970 tons with a speed of 32 knots. Average dimensions were 260 feet × 27feet × 9 feet. Armament: three 4-inch guns; two 21-inch torpedo-tubes.

Name	Builder	Allocated 'K' Name
Acasta	John Brown	*King*
Achates	John Brown	*Knight*
Ambuscade	John Brown	*Keith*
Ardent	Denny	*Kenric*
Christopher	Hawthorn Leslie	*Kite*
Cockatrice	Hawthorn Leslie	*Kingfisher*
Contest	Hawthorn Leslie	*Kittiwake*
Fortune	Fairfield	*Kismet*
Garland	Cammell Laird	*Kenwulf*
Hardy	Thornycroft	*Kelpie*
Lynx	Harland & Wolf	*Koodoo*
Midge	Harland & Wolf	*Keitola*
Owl	Harland & Wolf	*Killer*
Paragon	Thornycroft	*Katrine*
Porpoise	Thornycroft	*Kennington*
Shark	Swan Hunter	*Kestrel*
Sparrowhawk	Swan Hunter	*Kingsmill*
Spitfire	Swan Hunter	*Keppel*
Unity	Thornycroft	*Kinsale*
Victor	Thornycroft	*Kingston*

Ultimate disposal: *Lynx* was mined in the Moray Firth, 1915; *Ardent* and *Fortune* were sunk at Jutland, 1916; *Contest* was sunk by submarines in the Channel, 1917; *Paragon* was sunk by destroyers in the Channel, 1917; the others were sold 1920–23.

TABLE 13: The 'L' Class

Twenty-two ships, completed in 1913–15. Their average displacement was 1000 tons with a speed of 31 knots. Average dimensions were 269 feet × 27½ feet × 10½ feet. Armament: three 4-inch guns; one 12-pounder; four 21-inch torpedo-tubes.

Name	Builder	Original Name
Laertes	Swan Hunter	*Sarpedon*
Laforey	Fairfield	*Florizel*
Lance	Thornycroft	*Daring*
Landrail	Yarrow	*Hotspur*
Lark	Yarrow	*Haughty*
Lassoo	Beardmore	*Magic*
Laurel	White	*Redgauntlet*
Laverock	Yarrow	*Hereward*
Lawford	Fairfield	*Ivanhoe*
Legion	Denny	*Viola*
Lennox	Beardmore	*Portia*
Leonidas	Harland & Wolf	*Rob Roy*
Liberty	White	*Rosalind*
Linnet	Yarrow	*Havock*
Llewellyn	Beardmore	*Picton*
Lochinvar	Beardmore	*Malice*
Lookout	Thornycroft	*Dragon*
Louis	Fairfield	*Talisman*
Loyal	Denny	*Orlando*
Lucifer	Harland & Wolf	*Rocket*
Lydiard	Fairfield	*Waverley*
Lysander	Swan Hunter	*Ulysses*

Ultimate disposal: *Louis* was wrecked in Suvla Bay, 1915; *Lassoo* was mined in the North Sea, 1916; *Laforey* was mined in the Channel, 1917; others all sold 1921–22.

to although, for the first time, two spares were to be embarked. The resulting class was the 'Acastas', of which twelve were built to the standard Admiralty design and eight were specials in various aspects. In order to speed the delivery of some of these boats for trial purposes, day and night shifts were worked on the *Acasta* herself, *Christopher* and *Shark* but their hurried completion appears to have resulted in an inferior product.

Displacement was 940 tons for the standard ships with Parsons turbines in all except the *Acasta*, *Achates* and *Ambuscade* built by John Brown, which as always had Brown-Curtis. Costs ranged from £97,307 for the last two named up to £104,779 for Swan Hunter's *Shark*, although this included gun mountings, torpedo-tubes and trials. The speeds were very varied on trials, the fastest being the *Christopher* with 33·1 knots, although this was on the Maplin course. Poorest performance was turned in by the *Contest* with 29·6. All had the Yarrow boiler.

Of the eight specials the *Hardy* was designed for 32 knots—all the others for 29; she was built by Thornycroft and launched in October 1912. She just failed to make her designed speed on full-power trials in 1913. The *Ardent* was the first destroyer to be framed on the longitudinal system;* she was contracted to Parsons with her hull constructed by Cammell Laird and she had semi-geared turbines which gave her 30 knots-plus.

The principle behind longitudinal framing is explained by Kenneth Poolman in his book *The Kelly*:

> The framework of a warship's hull is based on an arrangement of intersecting girders. These are disposed so that some run fore-and-aft, parallel to the keel of the ship, and are called either 'longitudinals' (those at the bottom of the ship's hull) or 'stringers' (those at the sides of the hull) while others, called 'frames', are set transversely or athwart-ships. In the old system the frames were in the majority, the longitudinals and stringers being, though fewer, of necessity 'deeper', i.e. wider in section, than the frames. In the new system the order was reversed. The longitudinals and stringers were greatly increased, and the frames decreased in number, while this time the frames were made deeper. This was called the 'longitudinal

---

* Longitudinal framing was not *generally* adopted in British destroyers until the 'J' Class of 1939.

system'. The idea, which was an adaptation of the Isherwood system of design previously used in the construction of tankers, was intended to provide a stiffer hull against the hard knocks of sea-time and possible enemy action—an important consideration in the construction of a destroyer, which is in the front line of naval warfare and spends nearly all her life at sea.

The *Ardent* was built as a prototype for the two-funnelled section of the 'L' Class which was to follow and she differed from the other 'Acastas' in having two funnels of equal height. Similarly the *Fortune,* built by Fairfields, was the test model for the three-funnelled members of the 'L' Class. She had a distinctive clipper bow which was unique and carried her 'Q' gun on a platform between Numbers 2 and 3 funnels. The other Thornycroft specials —*Paragon, Porpoise, Unity* and *Victor*—had a designed speed of 31 knots, but none of them achieved it on trial.

On their completion the 'Acastas' joined the 4th Flotilla with the Grand Fleet and remained in that unit throughout the war although by late 1916 the flotilla was no longer employed in the front line. In 1913 Winston Churchill became First Lord of the Admiralty and, with his passion for detail, set up a committee under Captain H. Lynes to thrash out a standard naming policy for destroyers, great numbers of which were envisaged in the worsening situation. In order to produce some uniformity within the flotilla the committee suggested that all existing destroyers should be formed into distinct classes and named by letters of the alphabet. The surviving 27-knotter destroyers were allotted to the 'A' Class, but the 30-knotters were so numerous that in order to accommodate them all they were split into three separate classes: the four-, three- and two-funnelled vessels of this group were allocated the letters 'B', 'C' and 'D' respectively; only the last group had any real resemblance to a class having all been constructed by the same firm, but it was expected that these boats would be phased out for scrapping within a short time and so this was accepted.

The system was carried through all the remaining classes right up to the brand-new 'Acastas', the 'Rivers' becoming the 'E' Class, the 'Tribals' or 'Oceans' the 'F', 'G' was the 'Beagles', 'H' the 'Acorns', 'I' the 'Acherons' and 'K' the 'Acastas'. The letter 'J' was omitted because of lack of suitable numbers of names beginning with this letter. It was proposed that all the destroyers of these groups should forthwith be renamed with their class letter. Lists of names were duly prepared but only the 'Acastas' had actually adopted them before the Admiralty decided that the corrections involved would be too many. The 'K' names allotted to the 'Acastas' in October 1913 were also dropped after a short time as the ships had almost all completed, but the following class, the 'Florizels' named mainly after characters in Scott and Shakespeare were all renamed at the same time.* It was an unfortunate step which entailed the loss of many fine, traditional destroyer names and almost at once broke down when the 'M' Class of over a hundred units was laid down in 1914. Subsequent wartime alterations to this class soon used up all the suitable 'M' names. Naming by class letters was continued as long as destroyers were built, with the even more untraditional exceptions of the 'Battle' and 'Weapons' Classes of 1944–8, which were given a dreary mixed bag of names.

$$*\quad*\quad*\quad*\quad*$$

During the first winter of the war the 4th Flotilla experienced much bad weather which led to helm-jamming in the *Lynx*. Detailed examinations were made but did not save her from becoming a loss early in the war. The 4th Flotilla's first major action took place on 16th December 1914 during the bombardment of Scarborough. The German High Seas Fleet was out in support of Hipper's battle cruisers and the Grand Fleet also sailed on the expectation of a big operation. Two divisions of the 4th Flotilla left Cromarty on the night of the 15th to rendezvous and it was these, led by Commander R. Parry in the *Lynx*, who stumbled across an enemy destroyer in the half-light of early morning.

The German boat turned and just after 0500 a stern chase commenced with the destroyers of both sides opening fire. Almost at once the *Lynx* was hit and her forward magazine flooded. At this juncture her troublesome helm jammed to starboard and she swung away from the pursuit of the enemy. Still under heavy fire the remainder of the flotilla followed her round showing that amazing inflexibility which appeared in the battle cruisers at Dogger Bank and in most of the ships at Jutland. The old maxim

* The 'K' names allocated to the 'Acastas' and the original names of the 'L' Class are given in Tables 12 and 13, pages 142 and 143.

of 'going for the enemy' had apparently been stifled over the last century by increasingly rigid adherence to the 'Book' so that even with the enemy in sight ahead the destroyers blindly followed their damaged leader out of the fight.

As they turned, the *Ambuscade* received a shell and suffered heavy damage; minutes later the confused flotilla was illuminated by the German cruiser *Hamburg* which at once opened a heavy fire on the *Hardy*. *Hardy* replied by firing a torpedo and the German ship turned away into the darkness again.

A brief lull followed during which time the damaged *Ambuscade* limped off home on her own in the darkness and the *Unity* stood by the *Lynx* as she got under way. The *Shark* (Commander Loftus Jones) meanwhile led off the rest of the division, *Acasta*, *Spitfire* and the damaged but mobile *Hardy*—she had been hit and had to steer from her secondary position in the engine room, but she kept in line at 25 knots.

This abbreviated formation almost at once ran into four or five enemy destroyers which were sighted to the eastward and the *Shark* led off in pursuit until, for the second time, they were led into the guns of a covering German cruiser squadron. Accurate fire from these drove the four British boats away, but not before the *Shark* had got off a sighting report timed at 0705 which read:

> Position 54.22 N. 3.20 E. Am keeping touch with large cruiser *Roon* and five destroyers steering east.

Some seventy minutes later the *Shark* again sent in a report:

> Am being chased to westward.

Unfortunately neither of these signals was received by Admiral Warrender's Battle Squadron until long after transmission, nor did Admiral Beatty with the battle cruisers receive notification in time. In fact, what the 4th Flotilla's feeble little destroyer force had tackled was nothing less than the outriders of the High Seas Fleet under Admiral Hipper with battleships, battle cruisers, light cruisers, three flotillas of destroyers and the armoured cruisers *Roon* and *Prinz Heinrich* as well.

Lynx was repaired but was lost almost immediately after recommissioning when she was mined off the Moray Firth on 9th August 1915. The others took their places in the flotilla and on 31st May were rewarded by taking part in the Battle of Jutland. Most of the flotilla was present, led by the coal-burning flotilla leaders *Tipperary* and *Broke*. Those in action were the *Acasta* (Lieutenant-Commander J. Barron), *Achates* (Commander R. Hutchinson), *Ambuscade* (Lieutenant-Commander G. Coles), *Christopher* (Lieutenant-Commander F. Kerr), *Contest* (Lieutenant-Commander E. Master), *Garland* (Lieutenant-Commander R. Goff), *Porpoise* (Commander H. Colville), *Shark* (Commander L. Jones), *Sparrow-hawk* (Lieutenant-Commander S. Hopkins), *Spitfire* (Lieutenant-Commander C. Trelawney) and *Unity* (Lieutenant-Commander A. Leeky). Of these boats the *Acasta*, *Christopher* and *Shark* were screening the three battle cruisers of Admiral Hood's 3rd Battle Cruiser Squadron.

These three boats, together with the *Ophelia*, a newly-commissioned 'M', were stationed on the port bow of the 3rd Battle Cruiser Squadron when, at 1750, they sighted the light cruisers and destroyers of Hipper's force forging up in pursuit of the *Chester*. Commander Loftus Jones determined to attack the *Regensburg* and her ten destroyers before they could manoeuvre to fire torpedoes at Hood's squadron. At full speed the four little boats closed the enemy and the range was soon down to 15,500 yards.

Just after 1800 the *Shark* and the *Acasta*, both under smothering fire from the German 2nd Scouting Squadron, each managed to fire a torpedo at the *Regensburg* forcing her away. But as the *Shark* turned the German fire took effect and she was heavily hit; her steering gear was shot away and her boiler oil feed pipes were severed. Within a short while she had slid to a halt, a stationary target for the German light cruisers and destroyers.

A heavy shell struck the fo'c'sle blowing the 4-inch gun over the side and killing its entire crew. The *Acasta* was also damaged but seeing her companion in trouble Lieutenant-Commander Barron took his ship alongside the *Shark* and offered to take her in tow. In the whirlwind of fire it is doubtful whether this would have been possible and Loftus Jones ordered the *Acasta* to rejoin Admiral Hood and added: 'Don't get sunk for us'. *Acasta* pulled away and the *Shark*'s crew settled at their posts to await the inevitable outcome. A brief respite was given by the appearance of the cruiser *Canterbury* which drew off the enemy cruisers, but once she had gone the two enemy destroyers closed for the kill. Only the midship 4-inch gun remained in use and Jones went down from the bridge and saw that the rafts were lowered into the water together with any other life-saving equipment; all the boats were shot to splinters. Collision mats were placed over the worst shell holes and all the men not engaged at the solitary gun were ordered to lie flat.

Expecting little resistance the enemy destroyers commenced firing and quickly closed the range down to a point-blank 600 yards. The *Shark* was hit on the after gun mount and then the bridge; Loftus Jones had one leg shot away at the knee. Despite this he continued to direct the gun as best he could from the after deck. With almost its final shots 'Q' Gun scored hits on both enemy destroyers and they drew off to 1,500 yards' range and deliberately fired torpedoes into the battered hulk of the *Shark*. One struck her amidships and she sank at once with all save five of her crew. Commander Jones died in the water through loss of blood; he was awarded a posthumous Victoria Cross in recognition of one of the most gallant destroyer fights of all time.

Unknown to Jones or his crew the German destroyer *V.48* had been hit so severely that she later sank with all hands; *Shark*'s sacrifice had not been in vain.

Meanwhile the *Acasta* had prowled away and found herself in the path of the badly battered ships of Hipper's battle cruiser force, who were themselves under heavy fire from the battleships of the Grand Fleet. Lieutenant-Commander Barron thereupon decided to attack in company with the *Ophelia* and at 4,500 yards they both fired and thought they had scored a hit on the *Lützow*; in fact what they saw striking her was a heavy shell.

It was not to be expected that such audacity would be ignored by Hipper's leviathans and the *Acasta* was deluged with the spray of shells from every manner of craft in Hipper's force. For almost half-an-hour she dodged in and out of the walls of spray and shrapnel, but finally she took a heavy shell in the engine room which killed five men and cut off power. Another hit shot away the steering gear and the *Acasta* came to a halt, out of control and right in the path of the Grand Fleet. She had a nervous time as division upon division of battleships roared past her, intent on battle. She finally managed to get under way at slow speed and after a hazardous night when she was twice fired on by German cruisers, the *Nonsuch* towed her safely in to Aberdeen.

The German Fleet escaped destruction in the poor visibility and Jellicoe decided not to attempt to decide the issue in a night action.

The remaining destroyer flotillas were stationed astern the Grand Fleet Battle Squadrons but were given absolutely no information about the dispositions of their own battle cruiser or light cruiser squadrons; they had therefore the extreme disadvantage of having first to ascertain whether the ships sighted that night were friendly or hostile. The Germans appear to have been better served by their leaders and had not the slightest hesitation in opening fire at once.

Thus it was that when Scheer began to edge his fleet eastwards during the night the only vessels barring his way were the scattered British destroyer flotillas; and the ships of the 4th were the first units his heavy ships met. The British ships were in line ahead in two divisions, *Tipperary* leading the *Spitfire, Sparrowhawk, Garland* and *Contest* followed by *Broke* leading the *Achates, Ambuscade, Ardent, Fortune, Porpoise* and *Unity*.

At 2030 the *Tipperary* sighted what was taken to be a British light cruiser squadron of three ships. They were in fact German and at 800 yards range they suddenly illuminated the *Tipperary* and blew her asunder in a deluge of fire. The next astern, *Spitfire*, at once turned towards the enemy line and fired two torpedos at a four-funnelled cruiser, the *Rostock*, one of which hit and so damaged the German ship that she later had to be sunk.

In an attempt to divert some of the fire from his leader, Lieutenant-Commander Trelawney then opened fire with his 4-inch guns. In this *Spitfire* succeeded only too well and was hit, her torpedo reloading gear being put out of action. Trelawney turned to the west thinking there was another British flotilla in that direction to give support, but instead he ran full tilt into the German Battle Fleet.

Two of the battleships shone their searchlights upon the blazing *Tipperary* and, taking them to be light cruisers, Trelawney opened fire on them extinguishing both lights. They belonged in fact to the battleships *Nassau* and *Westfalen*. Amazed no doubt at such impudence the 20,000 ton *Nassau* put her helm over to crush her puny assailant. Two shells from her secondary armament actually passed through *Spitfire*'s bridge-screens as the two ships closed, one took off Trelawney's cap and wounded him in the head, the other killed everyone on the bridge save Trelawney, the coxswain and one seaman.

With a collision imminent, *Spitfire*'s captain ordered her engines full ahead and put the helm hard over. It was not a moment too soon and the German battleship, instead of slicing the destroyer in half, struck her a glancing blow against her port bow. As they struck the *Nassau* depressed her 11-inch guns to their lowest limit and fired a full salvo. The range was nil and the shells passed well above the tiny destroyer, but the blast effect was shattering. *Spitfire*'s bridge and funnels were demolished completely and she was dismasted and her port boats destroyed. The ruined structure started burning, but strangely enough no other enemy homed on to the beacon.

Investigations were commenced to find out the full extent of the damage and Trelawney himself was given up as lost. The fo'c'sle was ripped open above the waterline for a length of some sixty feet and some 20 feet of armoured plating from the *Nassau* was left in the enormous gap. Amazingly the *Spitfire* was not taking water very severely, three of the boilers were found usable and the after steering position was connected up in readiness for the voyage home, a distance of some 260 miles. While they were thus engaged the *Spitfire* was almost run down by the blazing armoured cruiser *Black Prince* which missed them by a few feet. One account described this incident:

> She tore past us with a roar, rather like a motor roaring up-hill on low gear, and the very crackling and heat of the flames could be heard and felt. She was a mass of fire from foremast to mainmast, on deck and between decks. Flames were issuing out of her from every corner.

This was the last seen of that tragic vessel, which had mistaken the German dreadnoughts for British and had then been torn apart by their concentrated salvoes; she was another casualty of the appalling lack of information supplied this night to the British vessels. After the narrow escape, the *Spitfire*, little more than a floating wreck, was got under way and after a long thirty-six hour haul on her own made the Tyne under her own steam. Her casualties were six killed.

The third ship of the line, the *Sparrowhawk*, had also managed to discharge a torpedo when the *Tipperary* was hit, but then, having lost the *Spitfire*, she joined up astern of the *Broke*. She had also made a torpedo attack on the German ships and while shaping up to make another was caught by searchlight and at once subjected to smothering fire which completely wrecked her lower bridge.

With her helm jammed to starboard the *Broke* turned a half circle and sliced into the *Sparrowhawk* at full tilt, her knife-edge bows penetrating through the little destroyer's frail plating just forward of the bridge. Locked together the two ships came to a sudden halt. The enemy had ceased firing and after a short interval the *Broke* was able to go astern and started back towards the Tyne. At this instant the *Contest* came roaring out of the night and struck the *Sparrowhawk*, cutting some five feet off her stern and jamming her rudder to port. The *Sparrowhawk* was induced, at slow speed, to steer a westerly course using her propellers. Once they were investigated by a German destroyer from a hundred yards range but her commander appeared satisfied that the floating wreck was finished and backed off and left them. They struggled on without making much headway and around 0200 they sighted a German cruiser making straight for them. The torpedo-tubes and after gun were manned in readiness but when still some distance away the German vessel, probably the *Elbing* which had been badly damaged, turned over and sank.

Eventually, after rescuing some of *Tipperary*'s survivors, *Sparrowhawk* contacted the *Marksman* who attempted to tow them in. After attempts had been made it was decided reluctantly that she was beyond salvage and her crew were taken off before she was sunk by gunfire.

Both the *Contest* and *Unity* lost touch with the remaining units of their flotilla, the former with her damaged stem retired to the north-east while the *Unity* eventually joined up with the 9th and 10th Flotillas to the eastward. The *Garland* had also fired a torpedo at the enemy fleet at some 800 yards range and then almost collided with *Sparrowhawk* herself, but after losing touch for a while she found *Contest* and retired to the north with her.

Achates and *Ambuscade* both turned to attack the German ships, the latter ship getting off two torpedoes, but Commander Hutchinson cancelled the order to fire as he thought that friendly cruisers were between him and the enemy vessels. Twenty minutes later the *Ambuscade* fired another two torpedoes but then both destroyers were driven off by German cruisers.

After a brief lull the German battleships were in sight again from the *Ardent* and her next astern, the *Fortune*, fired a torpedo;

Fortune was almost immediately overwhelmed by the fire of several large ships and reduced to a flaming charnel house from which there were but ten survivors. The time was around midnight when *Fortune* went down and during the same burst of firing the *Porpoise* took an 8-inch shell at the base of her after funnel, which demolished the wheel and telegraphs and killed several of her crew. The ship came to a standstill but her captain, Commander Colville, managed to get her after steering position rigged up and she limped off for the Tyne with damaged boilers and casualties. She eventually found the *Garland* and *Contest* who went in with her.

Immediately after *Fortune* had been blown asunder the *Ardent* (Lieutenant-Commander A. Marsden) had turned to port and increased speed to evade the furious fire which engulfed her companion. On resuming his position astern of what he assumed to be the *Ambuscade* Marsden found his bows being crossed by four German ships, either cruisers or battleships, and he at once fired his remaining torpedo.

Again, without hesitation, searchlights locked straight on to the *Ardent* and for five minutes two German vessels subjected the *Ardent* to an accurate shower of high explosive. At such close range the enemy could hardly fail to hit and they devastated the destroyer, her hull, funnels, bridge and upperworks shot through and through, the bulk of her crew dead or wounded with all her boats and rafts destroyed, her engines stopped, her armament wiped out.

There was a brief lull during which time Marsden, badly wounded, dragged himself aft, and then another group illuminated the stationary wreck and poured in further salvos until the *Ardent* turned over and sank. Some forty men including her captain got clear, but most died during the night and only Marsden and two others were alive when found by *Marksman* and *Obdurate* next day. Four officers and seventy-four men were dead.

In all the 4th Flotilla suffered the most grievous losses of any British destroyer unit in any war that day and night—462 men being casualties, excluding those lost in the *Acasta* and *Shark*. Of those ships of the 4th Flotilla which survived, all were repaired and back in service by the end of August.

It should be made clear here that the terrible carnage inflicted on the flotilla was in no way a reflection on the design or handling of the destroyers themselves. Surprising though this must appear, no ship in the British fleet was in any way prepared for a night encounter with the enemy. Jellicoe knew the dangers of this and it is for this reason that he declined to mix it with his battleships, preferring to wait for a morning encounter—which in fact never came. The lesson to be learned from this shambles was that allowance in training must be made for the unexpected; the post-war emphasis on night-fighting certainly reaped handsome dividends in the Second World War on many occasions, of which the Battle of Matapan is perhaps the best-known example.

In the latter part of the war the 'Acastas' were fitted out for anti-submarine duties and their armaments were much changed and specialised equipment added. The *Garland* was selected for anti-aircraft gun trials with the 4-inch Mark IV gun in September 1916. The most interesting experiment was made with the *Unity* which in April 1918 embarked an observation balloon for convoy escort duties. *Cockatrice* had depth charge racks and throwers fitted early in the same year while *Owl* embarked the first hydrophones with directional capability. In order to carry the required thirty depth charges, chutes and throwers most of the 'Ks' landed their after gun, both sets of tubes and sweep gear.

During a raid by German destroyers on the night of the 17th–18th March 1917 the *Paragon* was on her patrol line off Calais. On sighting three or four unknown craft *Paragon*'s captain made the required challenge and the reply was a torpedo which struck her amidships. She returned the fire and got off a single torpedo without effect; she herself sank within eight minutes of being hit. Her survivors were being rescued by the *Laforey* and *Llewellyn* when the enemy returned and torpedoed the latter. *Llewellyn* made port but only two of the *Paragon*'s crew survived.

The final casualty the 4th Flotilla was to take occurred on 18th September, also in the Channel, when the *Contest* was torpedoed and sunk.

The *Porpoise* was sold to Brazil after the war but all the other 'Acastas' went to the breakers in 1921–3.

Chapter X

Eve of Conflict

For the *Florizel* ordered under the 1912–13 Programme the Admiralty expressed a desire for a cheap ship to be basically an 'Improved Acasta' with three 4-inch semi-automatic guns, but she was to feature the new twin torpedo-tubes designed by boffins of the *Vernon*—which for the first time raised the torpedo armament of our new destroyers up to the standard of the German boats. Despite the slight improvements effected in speed since the 'Acorn' Class there was still some uneasiness at the two to three knot lead the Germans held over our boats. Despite this the average trial speed for these ships was 30 knots, although there were a few notable exceptions such as *Landrail* with $32\frac{1}{2}$ knots. However, due to the outbreak of war in 1914, many of these ships did not run official trials at all.

Displacement was 990 tons, length overall being 268 feet; the majority of the 'Florizel' or 'L' Class had Parsons turbines, but the *Laforey, Lawford, Louis, Lydiard, Lark, Landrail, Laverock* and *Linnet* had Brown-Curtis. The other notable advance was the fitting of the *Leonidas* and *Lucifer* with fully geared turbines—the first time these had been used. The average cost of these ships complete with armament was £120,900 which did not compare at all favourably with the German figure of £88,750.

Laurel and *Liberty*, from Whites, had three White Forster boilers, while *Lark, Landrail* and *Linnet* were fitted with three of Yarrow's own boilers. These five were known as the 'Two Funnelled Ls'. The remainder sported three funnels and were equipped with four Yarrow boilers. The *Lochinvar* and *Lassoo* were additions to the class ordered from Beardmores, under the Emergency War Programme, and not delivered until late in 1915. Their original, traditional names were changed to conform with the new alphabetical listing in October 1913.

The Yarrow-built *Laverock* disgraced herself by grounding on her way down the Clyde for trials on 27th February 1914 and compounded her misdeed by running hard aground on the rocks near the Skelmorlie run the next day. It was October before she completed repairs and trials. The bulk of these boats were completed on the outbreak of war and formed the 3rd Flotilla based on Harwich. The *Lance* joined on the 1st August bringing the strength up to a full sixteen boats. Pending the arrival of *Laverock*, the composition was as follows:

Light Cruiser:	*Amphion* (Captain C. H. Fox)
1st Division:	*Lance* (Commander W. de M. Egerton)
	Legion (Lieutenant-Commander C. F. Allsup)
	Lennox (Lieutenant-Commander C. R. Dane)
	Loyal (Lieutenant-Commander F. B. Watson)
2nd Division:	*Lark* (Commander R. G. Rowley-Conway)
	Landrail (Lieutenant-Commander B. L. Owen)
	Lookout (Commander A. B. S. Dutton)
	Lydiard (Lieutenant-Commander C. R. Hemans)
3rd Division:	*Laforey* (Commander G. R. L. Edwards)
	Lawford (Lieutenant-Commander A. A. Scott)
	Louis (Lieutenant-Commander R. W. U. Bayly)
	Leonidas (Lieutenant-Commander R. W. Grubb)
4th Division:	*Laurel* (Commander G. P. England)
	Liberty (Lieutenant-Commander R. B. C. Hutchinson, DSO)
	Lysander (Commander H. F. H. Wakefield)
	Laertes (Lieutenant-Commander M. L. Goldsmith)

* * * * *

The two flotillas based at Harwich adopted a set patrol routine in the opening months of the war. Each flotilla took it in turn to leave Harwich at around 0400 and proceed across the North Sea to relieve the other. Generally they took up a course and speed to pass the Terschelling Light Vessel, a famous mark for destroyer men in World War One, at around 1100. Here they would deploy by divisions during the day to cover a line from Heligoland to the mouth of the Ems River. Here they tried to surprise the enemy patrol lines and here, after dark, they formed their own line to prevent enemy destroyers slipping through to attack the packed troop transports taking the BEF into France.

As is well known the first recorded British shot in the First World War was fired by the destroyer *Lance* on 5th August—the gun which fired this shot is on display in the Imperial War Museum, London. This action took place when, in the course of a normal patrol, a fishing vessel reported to them that a steamer had been observed acting suspiciously, 'throwing things overboard' as it was put at the time, some thirty miles off Southwold in the vicinity of the Outer Gabbard Lightship.

The destroyers were spread in line of search and at 1000 the *Lance* and *Landrail* sighted the vessel which was identified as the fast mail-steamer *Königin Luise*. She ignored their order to heave-to and at 1100 the *Lance* opened fire followed by the *Landrail*. Within a short time the German ship was hit many times and set on fire. By noon she was clearly sinking and her crew were seen jumping overboard. At slow speed she kept moving through the water until she rolled over and sank. The two destroyers managed to rescue forty-three of the German crew with their boats.

Satisfaction for such an early success was soon marred for the following day the *Amphion* struck one of the German mines—for this is what the *Königin Luise* had been throwing overboard—and sank with heavy loss of life, including many of the German prisoners. As the little cruiser sank she hit a second mine and a shell from her hit the *Lark*, killing two of *Amphion*'s crew who had just been picked up. The *Linnet* was also hit by debris with the loss of one man.

The Battle of the Bight on 28th August has already been dealt with in some depth, but as the 'Ls' were well in the thick of the fighting it is necessary to return to it. The first action opened with the sighting and pursuit of the German destroyer *G.194* by the 4th Division. Despite their best efforts the German boat quite outpaced them. Further destroyers were duly sighted and the *Laurel* (Commander F. F. Rose) engaged them, driving them back on Heligoland. With the range at 7,000 yards the four British ships swept through the inner patrols damaging several small German torpedo-boats as they did so, but in the early morning haze—it was 0700—the shooting on both sides was ineffective.

Several enemy cruisers then appeared and the action became general with the *Arethusa* suffering many casualties but forcing the German *Frauenlob* to turn away. The fighting continued. Around noon, it appeared as if the German light cruiser *Mainz* was doomed and the 4th Division of the 3rd Flotilla was sent in from 5,000 yards to attack her with torpedoes. Although in a hopeless position the German vessel's gunnery was in no way impeded and she proceeded to dish out, to the 4th Division and other boats, some very rough treatment.

Laurel fired two torpedoes from a thousand yards and was then hit hard while turning away. One shell penetrated her boiler room killing four men, another detonated the lyddite, shells and charges when it struck her midships gun platform; the resultant explosion partially demolished the after funnel. A third hit was taken on the fore gun killing three of the gun crew. Her captain was wounded twice and she was taken out of the action, badly damaged, by her First Lieutenant, C. R. Peploe. *Laurel* was later brought in safely under tow of the *Amethyst* from Harwich.

The next in line was the *Liberty*; partially hidden by *Laurel*'s smoke, she fired two torpedoes but on turning away she was exposed to the *Mainz* who shifted target to her and almost at once scored a devastating hit on her bridge. Her foremast, binnacle and searchlight were carried away and her captain was killed. Two further shells burst through her crew space without exploding. Again it was her First Lieutenant, H. E. Horan, who took over the ship and kept her in action.

The *Lysander* avoided a full salvo aimed at her by turning to avoid hitting the *Liberty*. She fired both torpedoes at the *Mainz* then turned her attentions to another cruiser sighted coming up. The fourth destroyer in line, the *Laertes*, took a full salvo of four shells and was brought to a standstill heavily damaged. In addition the first shot from her foremost gun burst in the barrel. With her boilers out of action, she was towed home by the *Fearless*; her casualties were two killed and six wounded.

There was no lack of action and on the 17th October the *Undaunted* led the *Lance, Lennox, Legion* and *Loyal* in a sweep off the Island of Texel where they rolled up a German patrol flotilla. The enemy ships were first sighted in the early afternoon, hull down some sixty miles west of Texel. The Germans were steaming south when first sighted and line ahead was ordered to overhaul them. Once the British force was sighted the German boats turned east but to no avail. The destroyers were disposed two ahead and two astern the *Undaunted* and gradually overhauled the enemy squadron.

At long range the 6-inch guns of the *Undaunted* hit and slowed down the enemy ships who, realising that escape was out of the question, turned in an attempt to torpedo her. The British cruiser soon despatched the *S.119*, and a little while later the *S.117* was also blasted to the bottom by 6-inch shells at point-blank range. The British destroyers in pairs took on the remaining two Germans. The *Loyal* was hit in the stern and her after 4-inch gun put out of action, while the *Legion* took a shell into the bridge which put her steering gear out of action, but in a short while the *S.118* and *S.115* were both despatched. Only thirty-one German sailors survived from the four ships.

During the bombardment of Yarmouth on 23rd November the *Undaunted* with the *Laurel, Legion, Lennox* and *Lysander* and the *Aurora* with the *Lark, Lawford* and *Laverock* were at sea on a raid against German minesweepers. Joined by the *Landrail* these two units were for a period steaming parallel courses less than ten miles apart from Hipper's battle cruisers, but no sightings were made on either side.

At the Battle of the Dogger Bank the *Liberty* took the damaged *Meteor* in tow to Immingham. On 24th March 1915 the Harwich Force—*Arethusa, Aurora, Undaunted* and sixteen destroyers of the 3rd and 10th ('M' Class) Flotillas—were at sea escorting the seaplane carrier *Vindex* for a raid on the German base of Borkum. At midnight thick fog descended and the mission was called off, but in the complicated process of turning the whole force 8 points to starboard at 10 knots with visibility nil, the columns became bunched up and the *Landrail*, having missed the signal for the first of two 90 degree turns, lost touch with her next ahead. Being stationed on the inner side of the wheel to port she continued on and crossed the line of the cruisers.

She struck the *Undaunted* at right angles penetrating deeply into the cruiser's port quarter, doing considerable damage to the hull and upper deck and wrecking the twin torpedo-tubes. Fortunately the warheads did not explode but even so the gash in her hull was serious and several men were killed.

Undaunted was able to steam away under her own power; not so the *Landrail*. The destroyer's fo'c'sle was crushed in for a length of some twenty or thirty feet by the impact and the forepart of her deck collapsed into the hole until the stem almost touched the water. Luckily her forward mess decks were empty at the time.

After shoring up the damage as best they could the *Landrail* started for home at slow speed, but after a while her forward bulkheads started showing signs of strain and an oil tank began leaking.

At 0800, some two hours after the collision, engines were stopped and every means was found of lightening the ship forward, ammunition being transferred aft and fitments torn out to bring her bows up. The fog remained, but for a time *Landrail* was able to steam west at 10 knots. Two hours later the *Arethusa* and *Aurora* with two divisions of destroyers returned to find the lone cripple and afford some degree of safety as the fog began to lift.

However, the weather worsened during the morning and speed was progressively reduced. When it was clear that a gale was blowing up the *Landrail* was taken in tow by the *Mentor* but, as the sea grew rougher, the tow became unmanageable and finally parted. Both *Aurora* and *Arethusa* tried towing. The gale now arrived and during the long night the tow parted again and again as they steered for the Haisborough Channel. It was not until late the following morning, some seventy-two hours after she had been injured, that the *Landrail* was taken by tugs into the Nore. It was an epic struggle. Accidents of this nature grew ever more frequent as the war progressed, which was not surprising considering the flotillas went to sea regardless of conditions.

In 1915 the *Laforey, Lawford, Louis* and *Lydiard* went out to the Dardenelles for a time, taking part, among other duties, in the eventual evacuation of 'W' Beach. The *Louis* drove ashore in Suvla Bay on 31st October 1916 and became a total wreck.

Further casualties were sustained in the Harwich Force during the spring of 1915. When the *Recruit* was torpedoed by the *U.66* off the Galloper Shoal in the Thames Estuary on 1st May, the trawler *Daisy*, after picking up twenty-seven survivors, radioed for assistance and the duty division of the 3rd Flotilla, *Laforey, Lark, Lawford* and *Leonidas* under the command of Commander G. Edwards in the first-named, were despatched to search for the submarine.

They failed to find her after a long search, but while off the North Hinder Lightship they sighted two German torpedo-boats; the enemy boats had just sunk a patrol trawler and were chasing another. The *A.2* and *A.6*, they had sortied from Zeebrugge, and on sighting *Laforey*'s division attempted to make good their escape, but the 'Ls' were easily able to outpace them. The German ships, of 140 tons with a speed of 19 knots and mounting a single 2-inch gun each, were completely outclassed and both were quickly despatched without injury to the destroyers. Some fifty-seven survivors were picked up.

On 11th February 1916, when the *Arethusa* was mined, the *Loyal* attempted a tow but without success. The *Llewellyn* was damaged in a collision on 27th February, and the *Lennox* collided with the *Miranda* on the night of 9th–10th March but both got in under their own power.

A more serious accident occurred on 25th March. The Harwich Force with four light cruisers, the seaplane carrier *Vindex* and twenty-four destroyers sailed on the 23rd to carry out a bombardment of the Zeppelin sheds at Tondern on the landward side of the Isle of Sylt. A division of destroyers under the *Mansfield*— with the *Medusa*, *Murray* and *Laverock*—was sent on ahead to clear up the German patrol line and soon stumbled on several trawlers. They settled down to sinking them; two had been put down and a third was being purused when the *Laverock* struck the *Medusa* in the engine room holing her badly and putting her engines out of action. Fortunately, although her bows were severely damaged, *Laverock* made port under her own power.

A division of the 'Ls' was in action at Jutland in May with the 9th Flotilla screening the 2nd Battle Cruiser Squadron. The boats involved were *Landrail*, *Laurel*, *Liberty* and *Lydiard* but, humiliatingly, they were unable to keep up the speed of Beatty's great ships and had to fall back under the protection of the 5th Battle Squadron as their funnel smoke was obscuring the British ships' rangefinders. The *Laurel* rescued fourteen survivors from the *Queen Mary*—which had blown up—but they never got into the action. Only slight damage was received from shell splinters.

On 13th August 1916 the *Lance*, *Laverock*, *Lassoo* and other destroyers were escorting a small convoy to Holland when the *Lassoo* (Lieutenant-Commander V. S. Butler) struck a mine off the Mass Light Vessel. The mine exploded abreast the after bank of torpedo-tubes, the ship's back was broken and she split in half, four men being lost. At first a submarine attack was suspected, and *Laverock*'s sweep was in fact exploded, but this was later thought to have been set off as it fouled a wreck. All save a dozen of the crew were taken aboard the *Lance* and Lieutenant-Commander Butler went below to organise the shoring up of the after bulkhead in the still floating fore portion of his vessel. The damage, however, proved too severe; within a short time the bulkheads collapsed, drowning one man, and thirty-five minutes after striking she went down.

A similar mishap took place in November when the *Legion* was mined aft; her shafts were twisted and her steering gear wrecked. Despite this she was brought home. She was refitted as a mine-laying destroyer—one of the first of her kind—and was so success-ful that her sisters *Lawford* and *Loyal* were also converted to carry forty mines with rails aft; the after gun and both banks of torpedo tubes were landed and a canvas screen erected to disguise this fact.

The surviving 'L' Class boats went to the Dover Patrol at the end of 1916 replacing the 'Tribals' and 'Rivers', their places being taken by the new 'M' and 'R' Class destroyers then joining the fleet. Here the *Llewellyn* became the first destroyer to sink a sub-marine with depth charges, being responsible for the destruction of the *UC.19* in the Straits on 4th December 1916.

On 1st March 1917 the *Laverock* was on patrol in the Channel when she was surprised by five German destroyers who hit her with a torpedo which luckily failed to explode. On the night of the 17th–18th when the *Paragon* was sunk, the *Laforey* and *Llewellyn* came on the scene and switched on their searchlights to hunt for survivors. Attracted by this the Germans who had attacked the *Paragon* returned and torpedoed the *Llewellyn* in the bows. She remained afloat although badly damaged and was brought back to Dover in tow minus her stem section. A week later *Laforey* came to grief on a minefield and sank, but this was their final casualty of the war.

Although only eight years old when the Washington Treaty came into force, the 'L' Class destroyers were nevertheless put on the sales list and by 1923 the last of them, *Lark*, had gone.

The 'L' Class boats, representing the final stage of destroyer development in this period, proved to be excellent ships in service; the hundreds of 'M', 'R' and 'S' Class boats which fol-lowed under the expanded war programmes were all built to this sound design and formed the solid backbone of the Grand Fleet flotillas. Later, in response to a German programme which never materialised, came the 'V' and 'W' Classes which were again a great stride forward both in size and design, but the success of the basic 'L' Class prototypes was emphasised by the durability and handiness of the 900-ton destroyer. In fact, although in much modified form, this design was the basis upon which the 'Hunt' Class destroyers of 1939 were built.

*   *   *   *   *

The sale of the *Lark* marks the end of the story of the first destroyers, the ships which were designed before the outbreak of the First World War. The rapid growth of the new weapon was the result of increasing naval rivalry which threatened Britain's long domination of the seas, coupled with the enormous technical strides made in marine engineering over the space of twenty short years. In that time the destroyer had grown from a tiny 240-ton racing midget of a boat to a tonnage four times that size. By 1914 a displacement of 1,000 tons, quite outrageously large when the 'Tribals' appeared, was the norm, while in Germany 2,000-tonners were on the drawing-boards. Armaments, complements and other gear had increased beyond all expectation in that same period, and yet the boats like the *Lurcher, Firedrake* and *Oak* which went to war in August 1914 were able to carry all this top hamper into battle at speeds which would have amazed those who took Alfred Yarrow's first frail creation to sea in 1893.

The development of the torpedo had continued throughout the twenty years covered by this volume and by the time the 'River' Class commissioned the standard weapon for the Royal Navy was the Mark V torpedo. This carried a 295-pound warhead and weighed 1,350 pounds. Heating of the pressurised air was introduced in 1907 with the Mark VII type and gave the weapon a range of 7,000 yards at 30 knots. The following year two new types were introduced, the 'Short' and the 'Modified Long' torpedoes. Both had a range of 1,000 yards at 50 knots with a maximum of 7,500 yards for the Short type and 12,000 for the Long.

Most surprising was the length of time taken to develop and fit a twin torpedo mounting, despite its obvious advantage of doubling the warload which could be delivered instantly. Problems of weight seem to have been mainly responsible for its delayed introduction into service. Again weight restrictions led to most pre-war destroyers going into action carrying only a single reload torpedo which meant that their usefulness in a prolonged engagement was strictly limited.

This limitation largely came about because British destroyers were always built with the emphasis on their 'preventive' role. The old idea of Torpedo Boat Destroyers still endured and indeed the title of Torpedo Boat Destroyer was not finally dropped until the 1920s. While the destroyer men themselves concentrated more on the offensive role of torpedoing the enemy battleships, there still existed the higher official viewpoint that this task was the responsibility of our own Battle Fleet and that the destroyers' task was still to shield our own battle-line. Indeed, until 1910 the torpoedoes for the Royal Navy were included under the Army Vote—not until that late date did the Naval Ordnance Department assume responsibility for this major weapon!

In gun development the two big armament firms of Armstrong and Vickers were responsible for the design and construction of the weapons themselves, although Woolwich Arsenal was the official source of supply. Again, the ever-increasing sizes of torpedo-craft called for heavier calibres of gun in British destroyers to counter them. The equipping of the earlier 'Tribals' with 12-pounders was manifestly absurd and an example of unnecessary resistance to change. Here Fisher was to blame for his insistence that larger guns would hamper destroyers in a pursuing role. In time of war it was soon shown that the 12-pounder was useless.

Conversely, of course, there was a limit to what was practical on such a lively gun-platform as a destroyer and experiments with a 6-inch gun on the *Swift* ended in failure. The Germans made a similar mistake during the Second World War. The adoption of the 4-inch gun was undoubtedly a major step forward and British destroyers thus equipped were proven superior to the German boats in fire-power.

Despite the many brilliant designs brought out, of which the Yarrow *Firedrake, Lurcher* and *Oak* were supreme examples, war service tended to show that, when it came to speed, the German boats invariably had the edge over the British destroyers in any engagement. However, in the majority of cases, this was not the fault of the design of British destroyers, but arose more because of the fact that the British ships were constantly employed at sea—with the resultant wear and tear, weather damage and like faults; the German destroyers on the other hand only put to sea with picked coal and crews in the most favourable circumstances. Thus the German boats were always at their peak of performance and employed on strictly limited objectives, always with the advantage of surprise. It is little wonder, then, that time and time again they seemed to possess qualities of gunnery, speed and resistance far superior to our own.

In fact, high speed, although desirable, was only needed in service on very rare occasions and the Admiralty's basic insistence on the greater value of staying power and seaworthiness proved in the long run to have been perfectly sound and valid. These qualities were thoroughly tested throughout the war and were not found wanting. The value of destroyers which could stay at sea under the most gruelling conditions of wind and weather far offset any lack of a knot or two's speed on the odd occasions when such a need arose. True, lack of speed in certain areas, notably on the Dover Patrol, led directly to several defeats and failures to stop the German hit-and-run raids; but here the fault surely lay in employing some of our oldest destroyers in defence of an area under attack from the Germans' newest and most powerful vessels. Once this unsound policy was reversed, the British destroyers proved equal to the task of policing the Straits. But over all, the Admiralty's policy of endurance rather than setting records was fully justified in both World Wars.

Every criticism of design during the years 1893–1913 must be tempered by the fact that these two decades were years of experiment in hull form, propulsion, armament and function for this new type of a warship; the lack of any major conflict in a period of such enormous change in the application of seapower made the Admiralty's task very difficult. The lessons of war showed up many failings, but on the whole the soundness of most of the adopted designs meant that the bulk of the destroyers of this period came through four gruelling years of war with very little alteration.

In fact, destroyers as a type required fewer major alterations than any other warship, although their duties grew almost daily as those of the battleship and cruiser declined. By this yardstick and despite some notable mistakes—poor armament in the huge 'Tribals', coal fuel for the 'Beagles' and the retention of single torpedo mounts are the most obvious—the British destroyer was far superior to the American boats of the same period and was the model for most of the other foreign designs. In conflict, if not on paper, they were to prove superior to the German destroyers also.

Much of the destroyers' duties were unknown or at least uncertain before 1914, and few people realised the extent to which they would dominate the subsequent war at sea. The battleship was still supreme; unrestricted mine warfare seemed unthinkable; and save for Fisher and a few likeminded men, the submarine menace remained undreamt. Experience of torpedo warfare was minimal and not impressive, but within a very few months it was shown just how much the mere threat of massed torpedo attack could impress itself upon those in high command.

In twenty years, 1893–1913, the destroyer had established itself; the pattern had emerged and would govern the design of subsequent classes for another forty years. But the destroyer story was by no means finished, for 1914 was the threshold of still more momentous achievements; for the time being, the uneasy years of world peace were over.

Composition of Flotilla in 1906

CHANNEL FLEET:
1st Flotilla Portsmouth:
Boyne Crane Derwent Doon Fawn Flirt Garry Kangaroo Myrmidon Peterel Ribble Waveney
2nd Flotilla Nore:
Earnest Exe Lively Ness Nith Orwell Seal Sprightly Swale Thrasher Ure Wear
3rd Flotilla Devonport:
Arab Arun Cheerful Express Foyle Greyhound Itchen Liffey Moy Ouse Racehorse Roebuck
Attached Vessels:
Sapphire (Depot Ship) *Sapphire II* (Tender) *Pathfinder Patrol Sentinel* (Scouts for Leaders) *Tyne* (Depot Ship)
MEDITERRANEAN FLEET:
4th Flotilla:
Albatross Angler Ardent Ariel Banshee Boxer Bruiser Foam Mallard Stag
Attached Vessel:
Vulcan (Depot Ship)
CHINA STATION:
Fame Hardy Hart Janus Otter Virago Whiting
IN COMMISSION IN RESERVE:
Nore Tenders to *Pembroke*:
Bullfinch Charger Cherwell Conflict Dee Dove Eden Erne Ettrick Hasty Havock Griffon (Gibraltar) *Hornet Locust Oppossum Panther Quail Ranger Rother Salmon Snapper Sunfish Teazer Wizard Wolf Zebra*
Nore Tenders to *Wildfire*:
Hardy Haughty
Nore Tender to *Actaeon*:
Dasher
Attached Vessels:
Leander (Depot Ship). *Adventure Attentive* (Scouts) *Jason Speedwell*

Speedy (Torpedo Gunboats)
Devonport Tenders to *Vivid*:
Bittern Blackwater Colne Contest Daring Fairy Falcon Ferret Gipsy Jed Kennet Lee Leopard Leven Lynx Mermaid Osprey Ostrich Spitfire Sturgeon Success Swordfish Sylvia Velox Vixen
Devonport Tenders to *Cambridge*:
Avon Violet
Devonport Tender to *Defiance*:
Starfish
Devonport Tender to *Britannia*:
Chelmer
Attached Vessels:
Skirmisher (Scout) *Circe* (Torpedo Gunboat)
Portsmouth Tenders to *Victory*:
Bat Brazen Coquette Cygnet Cynthia Electra Flying Fish Gala Hunter Kale Kestrel Lightning Recruit Shark Spiteful Star Surly Syren Teviot Thorn Tiger Usk Vigilant Vulture Welland Zephyr
Portsmouth Tenders to *Excellent*:
Ferret Porcupine
Portsmouth Tender to *Vernon*:
Rocket
Attached Vessels:
Hecla (Depot Ship) *Forward Foresight* (Scouts) *Spanker* (Torpedo Gunboat)

Pendant Numbers †

TABLE ONE: Classes A, B, C and D. As adopted in 1913
Section A: Classes A and B

	6-12-14	22-2-15	1-9-15	1-1-18	1-4-18	14-6-18	13-9-18	Alterations at various dates to 13-9-18
Arab	D01	D01	D77	D05	H08	H08	H08	H08
Boxer	H4C	H4C	H4C	D16	—	—	—	—
Bruiser	*	*	*	*	*	*	*	*
Conflict	P24	*	D96	D18	D18	D18	D18	D18
Earnest	D05	D05	D79	D29	D29	D29	D29	D29
Express	D84	D84	D80	D34	D34	D34	D34	D34
Fervent	N17	*	D97	D39	D39	D39	D39	D39
Griffon	D39	D39	D81	D45	D45	D45	D45	D45
Kangaroo	P02	*	D82	D48	D48	D48	D48	D48
Lightning	N23	*	—	—	—	—	—	—
Lively	D91	D91	D83	D53	D53	D53	D53	D53
Locust	D29	D29	D84	D54	D54	H02	H02	H02
Myrmidon	P83	*	D85	—	—	—	—	—
Opossum	D12	D12	D99	D62	D62	D62	D62	D62
Orwell	D49	D49	D86	D63	D63	D63	D63	D63
Panther	D69	D69	D87	D67	D67	D67	D67	D67
Peterel	P74	*	D88	D68	D68	D68	H54	H54
Porcupine	N19	*	D0A	D69	D69	D69	D69	D69
Quail	D85	D85	D89	D70	D70	D70	H32	H32
Ranger	*	*	D1A	*	*	*	*	*
Seal	D77	D77	D90	D75	D75	D75	D75	D75
Spiteful	P73	*	D91	D76	D76	D76	D76	*
Sprightly	D62	D62	D92	D77	D77	D77	D77	*
Success	D24	—	—	—	—	—	—	—
Sunfish	D47	D47	D2A	D81	D81	D81	D81	D81
Surly	P30	*	D3A	D82	D82	D82	D82	D82
Syren	P72	*	D93	D85	D85	D85	D85	D85
Thrasher	D79	D79	D94	D90	D90	D90	D90	D90
Wizard	H3C	H3C	H3C	H7A	H7A	H7A	H7A	H7A
Wolf	D98	D98	D95	D97	D97	D97	D97	D97
Zephyr	N86	*	D4A	D98	D98	D98	D98	D98

* Pendant Number either not issued for this period or untraceable in the records.
— No Pendant Number because ship was either lost or taken out of service.

† The missing sets of 1916–17 Pendants have been located too late for inclusion in this book.

ABLE ONE (*continued*)

ection B: Classes B and C

	6-12-14	22-2-15	1-9-15	1-1-18	1-4-18	14-6-18	13-9-18	Alterations at various dates* to 13-9-18
lbacore	P14	*	D76	Do1	Do1	Do1	Do1	Do1
neita	D15	D15	D78	D11	D11	D11	D11	D11
lbatross	D32	D32	D44	Do2	Do2	Do2	Do2	Do2
von	Do2	Do2	D45	Do8	Do8	Do8	Do8	Do8
t	P97	*	D46	Do9	Do9	Do9	H87	H87
tern	Do3	Do3	D5A	D10	D10	—	—	—
azen	N11	*	D47	D14	D14	D14	D14	D14
llfinch	D17	D17	D48	D15	Ho4	Ho4	Ho4	Ho4
heerful	P13	*	D49	—	—	—	—	—
ane	P26	*	D50	D20	D20	D20	H72	H72
ove	D34	D34	D51	D28	D28	D28	D28	D28
ectra	N55	*	D52	D31	D31	D31	D31	D31
airy	P40	*	D53	D35	D35	—	—	—
alcon	P31	*	D54	D36	—	—	—	—
awn	P94	*	D55	D38	D38	D38	H38	H38
irt	P87	*	D56	—	—	—	—	—
ving Fish	P86	*	D57	D40	D40	D40	H69	H69
ipsy	P23	*	D58	D43	D43	D43	D43	D43
reyhound	Po1	*	D59	D44	D44	D44	H43	H43
strel	N47	*	D60	D49	D49	D49	D49	D49
eopard	D75	D75	D61	D50	Ho6	Ho6	Ho6	Ho6
even	P33	*	D62	D51	D51	D51	D51	D51
ermaid	P35	*	D63	D56	D56	D56	H85	H85
prey	P80	*	D64	D64	D64	D64	D64	D64
trich	P56	*	D65	D65	D65	D65	D65	D65
ter	*	*	*	*	*	*	*	*
acehorse	P15	*	D66	D71	D71	D71	D71	D71
ecruit	N60	—	—	—	—	—	—	—
oebuck	D53	D53	D67	D72	D72	D72	D72	D72
ar	Po7	—	D68	D79	D79	D79	Ho7	Ho7
lvia	D23	D23	D69	D84	Ho3	Ho3	Ho3	Ho3
horn	D57	D57	D70	D89	D89	D89	D89	D89
elox	P45	*	D71	—	—	—	—	—
igilant	D43	D43	D72	D92	D92	D92	D92	D92
iolet	Do9	Do9	D73	D94	D94	D94	D94	D94
ixen	D44	D44	D74	D95	D95	D95	D95	D95
ulture	N50	*	D75	*	*	*	*	*

Pendant Number either not issued for this period or untraceable in the records.
- No Pendant Number because ship was either lost or taken out of service.

TABLE ONE (*continued*)
Section C: Class D

	6-12-14	22-2-15	1-9-15	1-1-18	1-4-18	14-6-18	13-9-18	Alterations at various dates to 13-9-18
Angler	P26	*	D36	D04	D04	D04	D04	D04
Coquette	N21	*	D37	—	—	—	—	—
Cygnet	N49	*	D38	D22	D22	D22	D22	D22
Cynthia	N09	*	D39	D23	D23	D23	D23	D23
Desperate	P50	*	D40	D26	D26	D26	D26	D26
Fame	*	*	*	D37	*	*	*	*
Mallard	D26	D26	D41	D55	D55	D55	D55	D55
Stag	P34	*	D43	D78	D78	D78	D78	D78

TABLE TWO: The 'River' Class

	6-12-14	22-2-15	1-9-15	1-1-18	1-4-18	14-6-18	13-9-18	Alterations at various dates to 13-9-18
Arun	N04	*	D11	D07	D07	D07	D07	D07
Boyne	N68	*	D12	D12	D12	D12	H23	H23
Chelmer	*	*	*	*	*	*	*	*
Cherwell	N90	*	D13	D17	D17	D17	D17	D17
Colne	*	*	*	*	*	*	*	*
Dee	N95	*	D14	D24	D24	D24	D24	D24
Derwent	N25	*	D15	—	—	—	—	—
Doon	N14	*	D16	D27	D27	D27	D27	D27
Eden	N42	*	D17	—	—	—	—	—
Erne	N58	—	—	—	—	—	—	—
Ettrick	N01	*	D18	D32	D32	D32	D32	D32
Exe	N05	*	D19	D33	D33	D33	H70	H70
Foyle	N44	*	D20	—	—	—	—	—
Garry	N10	*	D21	D41	D41	D41	H73	H73
Itchen	N06	*	D22	—	—	—	—	—
Jed	*	*	*	*	*	*	*	*
Kale	N45	*	D23	D47	—	—	—	—
Kennet	*	*	*	*	*	*	*	*

* Pendant Number either not issued for this period or untraceable in the records.
— No Pendant Number because ship was either lost or taken out of service.

ABLE Two: The 'River' Class—*Continued*

ffey	N07	*	D24	D52	D52	D52	D52	D52
by	N02	*	D25	D58	D58	D58	H76	H76
ss	N81	*	D26	D59	D59	D59	H77	H77
ith	N77	*	D27	D60	D60	D60	H78	H78
se	N69	*	D28	D66	D66	D66	H80	H80
bble	*	*	*	*	*	*	*	*
ther	N32	*	D29	D73	D73	D73	D73	D73
ale	N03	*	D31	D83	D83	D83	D83	D83
st	N34	*	D32	D87	D87	D87	H84	H84
viot	N26	*	D33	D88	D88	D88	D88	D88
e	N12	*	D34	D91	D91	D91	D91	D91
k	*	*	*	*	*	*	*	*
our	*	*	*	D80	D80	D80	H83	H83
aveney	N19	*	D35	D96	D96	D96	H86	H86
ear	*	*	*	*	*	*	*	*
elland	*	*	*	*	*	*	*	*

ABLE THREE: The 'Ocean' Class

	6-12-14	22-2-15	1-9-15	1-1-18	1-4-18	14-6-18	13-9-18	Alterations at various dates to 13-9-18
fridi	H40	H40	D00	D00	D00	D00	D00	D00
mazon	H37	H37	D01	D03	D03	D03	D03	D03
ssack	H09	H09	D02	D19	D19	D19	D19	D19
usader	H66	H66	D05	D21	D21	D21	D21	D21
burka	H52	H52	D04	—	—	—	—	—
aori	H16	H16	—	—	—	—	—	—
ohawk	H19	H19	D05	D57	D57	D57	D57	D57
ubian	H70	H70	D06	—	—	—	—	—
racen	H38	H38	D07	D74	D74	D74	D74	—
rtar	H29	H29	D08	D86	D86	D86	D86	D86
iking	H90	H90	D09	D93	D93	D93	D93	D93
lu	H86	H86	D10	—	—	—	—	—
ubian	*	*	*	D99	D99	D99	D99	D99

* Pendant Number either not issued for this period or untraceable in the records.
— No Pendant Number because ship was either lost or taken out of service.

TABLE FOUR: The 'Beagle' Class

	22-2-15	1-9-15	1-1-18	1-4-18	14-6-18	13-9-18	Alterations at various dates to 13-9-18	Early 1919
Basilisk	H89	*	*	*	*	*	*	H33
Beagle	*	*	HC5	HC5	HC5	HC5	HC5	H24
Bulldog	*	*	HC7	HC7	HC7	HC4	HC4	H25
Foxhound	*	*	H16	H16	H58	H58	H58	H26
Grampus	*	H07	H38		HA7	HA7	HA7	H31
Grasshopper	*	*	H17	H17	H60	H60	H60	H28
Harpy	D88	*	H19	H19	H71	H71	H71	H32
Mosquito	*	*	HA3	HA3	HA3	HA3	HA3	H29
Racoon	*	*	HA7	—	—	—	—	—
Rattlesnake	*	*	*	*	*	*	HC7	F96
Renard	*	*	*	*	*	*	H99	H27
Pincher	D87	*	*	HC2	HC2	—	—	—
Savage	D92	*	HA9	HA9	HA9	HA9	HA9	F97
Scorpion	D90	*		HC3	HC3	HC3	HC3	H30
Scourge	D96	*	H8A	H8A	H8A	H8A	H8A	F98
Wolverine	*	*	—	—	—	—	—	—

TABLE FIVE: The 'Acorn' Class

	6-12-14	22-2-15	1-9-15	1-1-18	Early 1919
Acorn	H02	H02	H02	H03	H64
Alarm	H05	H05	H05	H04	H96
Brisk	H18	H18	H70	H22	H65
Cameleon	H21	H21	H21	H24	H66
Comet	H25	H25	H25	—	—
Fury	H42	H42	H42	H35	H67
Goldfinch	H44	—	—	—	—
Hope	H48	H48	H48	H41	H68
Larne	H57	H57	H57	H50	H69
Lyra	H60	H60	H60	H67	H97
Martin	H65	H65	H65	H71	H21
Minstrel	H69	H69	H69	H88	H72
Nemesis	H72	H72	H72	H82	H73
Nereide	H74	H74	H74	H89	H70
Nymph	H83	H83	H83	D25	H98
Redpole	H77	H77	H77	H96	H71
Rifleman	H82	H82	H82	H97	H99
Ruby	H85	H85	H85	H98	H22
Sheldrake	H88	H88	H88	H0A	H23
Staunch	H89	H89	H89	—	—

* Pendant Number either not issued for this period or untraceable in the records.
— No Pendant Number because ship was either lost or taken out of service.

BLE SIX: The 'Acheron' Class

	6-12-14	22-2-15	1-9-15	1-1-18	Early 1919
heron	Hoo	Hoo	Hoo	Ho2	Ho5
cher	H10	H10	H29	Ho6	Ho6
iel	H11	H11	H37	Ho7	—
ack	H14	H14	H86	—	—
ger	H15	H15	H52	Ho9	H91
ver	H17	H77	H66	H20	Ho7
ender	H28	H28	H28	H29	H57
uid	H33	H33	H33	H30	H92
ret	H35	H35	H35	H32	H93
ester	H39	H39	H39	H34	H58
hawk	H45	H45	H45	H37	H59
ad	H47	H47	H47	H40	H60
rnet	H49	H49	H49	H42	Ho8
dra	H50	H50	H50	H43	H94
kal	H55	H55	H55	H44	H95
wing	H56	H56	H56	H48	Ho9
ard	H58	H58	H58	H60	H62
enix	H75	H75	H75	H94	—
dfly	H87	H87	H87	H99	H63
ress	H92	H92	H92	H4A	H61
edrake	H97	H97	H97	H33	H89
rcher	Ho1	Ho1	Ho1	H65	H90
e	H12	H12	H38	H92	H56

ABLE SEVEN: The 'Acasta' Class

	6-12-14	22-2-15	1-9-15	1-1-18	14-6-18 and 1-4-18	13-9-18	Alterations at various dates to 13-9-18	Early 1919
asta	H59	H59	H59	Hoo	Hoo	Hoo	Hoo	G40
hates	H46	H46	H46	Ho1	Ho1	Ho1	Ho1	Ho2
mbuscade	H62	H62	H62	Ho5	Ho5	Ho5	Ho5	H54
dent	H78	H78	H78	—	—	—	—	—
ristopher	H51	H51	H51	H25	H25	H25	H25	G58
katrice	H73	H73	H73	H26	H26	H26	H26	G57
ntest	H63	H63	H63	—	—	—	—	—
rtune	H30	H30	H30	—	—	—	—	—

Pendant Number either not issued for this period or untraceable in the records.
No Pendant Number because ship was either lost or taken out of service.

TABLE SEVEN: The 'Acasta' Class—*Continued*

Garland	H32	H32	H32	H36	H36	H36	H36	H5⋮
Hardy	H67	H67	H67	H39	H39	H39	H39	H8⋮
Lynx	H71	H71	—	—	—	—	—	—
Midge	H13	H13	H40	H79	H79	H79	H79	Ho⋮
Owl	H31	H31	H31	H93	H93	H93	H93	H8.
Paragon	H26	H26	H26	—	—	—	—	—
Porpoise	H27	H27	H27	H95	H95	H95	H95	H8(
Shark	Ho4	Ho4	Ho4	—	—	—	—	—
Sparrowhawk	H61	H61	H61	—	—	—	—	—
Spitfire	H41	H41	H41	H1A	H1A	H1A	H1A	H8⋮
Unity	H68	H68	H68	H5A	H5A	H5A	H5A	H8⋮
Victor	H36	H36	H36	H6A	H6A	H6A	H6A	Ho.

TABLE EIGHT: The 'L' Class

	6-12-14	22-2-15	1-9-15	1-4-18	14-6-18	13-9-18	Alterations at various dates to 13-9-18	Early 1919
Laertes	H94	H94	H94	H45	H45	H45	H45	H8c
Laforey	Ho3	Ho3	Ho3	—	—	—	—	—
Lance	H23	H23	H23	H46	H46	H46	H46	G96
Landrail	H54	H54	H54	H47	H47	H47	H47	H82
Lark	H34	H34	H34	H49	H49	H49	H49	Hoc
Laurel	H91	H91	H91	H51	H51	H51	H51	G98
Laverock	H53	H53	H53	H52	H52	H52	H52	G93
Lawford	Ho6	Ho6	Ho6	H53	H53	H53	H53	G94
Legion	H79	H79	H79	H54	H54	H54	H54	G95
Lennox	H95	H95	H95	H55	H55	H55	H55	Ho1
Leonidas	H20	H20	H20	H56	H56	H56	H56	H51
Liberty	H81	H81	H81	H57	H57	H57	H57	G99
Linnet	H43	H43	H43	H59	H59	H59	H59	H53
Llewellyn	H99	H99	H99	H61	H61	H61	H61	H83
Lookout	H24	H24	H24	H62	H62	H62	H62	G97
Louis	Ho7	Ho7	*	—	—	—	—	—
Loyal	H80	H80	H80	H63	H63	H63	H63	H50
Lucifer	H22	H22	H22	H64	H64	H64	H64	H52
Lydiard	Ho8	Ho8	Ho8	H66	H66	H66	H66	G48
Lysander	H93	H93	H93	H68	H68	H68	H68	H81
Lassoo	—	—	Go1	—	—	—	—	—
Lochinvar	—	—	Go6	F52	F52	F52	F52	H49

* Pendant Number either not issued for this period or untraceable in the records.
— No Pendant Number because ship was either lost or taken out of service.